SCRIPTURE TEXTBOOKS FOR CATHOLIC SCHOOLS

VOLUME V

THE KINGDOM OF PROMISE

SCRIPTURE TEXTBOOKS FOR CATHOLIC SCHOOLS

General Editor:
The Right Reverend Monsignor JOHN M. T. BARTON,
D.D., L.S.S., F.S.A. F.R.S.A.
English Consultor of the Pontifical Biblical Commission
Past President (1952), Society for Old Testament Study

THE KINGDOM OF PROMISE

Its preparation, foreshadowing and fulfilment

by

ROBERT A. DYSON, S.J., S.T.D., L.S.S.

*Professor of Old Testament Exegesis in the
Pontifical Biblical Institute, Rome*

AND

ALEXANDER JONES, S.T.L., L.S.S.

*Professor of Sacred Scripture at
Upholland College, Lancashire*

With a Foreword by His Eminence
THE CARDINAL ARCHBISHOP OF WESTMINSTER

SECOND EDITION

LONDON
BURNS & OATES LTD
MACMILLAN & CO LTD
1961

First Edition 1947
Reprinted 1951
Second Edition 1961

BURNS AND OATES LTD
28 *Ashley Place London SW*1

MACMILLAN AND COMPANY LIMITED
London Bombay Calcutta Madras Melbourne

THE MACMILLAN COMPANY OF CANADA LIMITED
Toronto

ST MARTIN'S PRESS INC
New York

Printed in Great Britain by
W & J Mackay & Co Ltd, Fair Row, Chatham

FOREWORD

THE present series of Scripture textbooks for schools is both welcome and opportune. The books ought to arouse a more intelligent interest in the minds of the children in the unspeakable treasures which God unfolds in His written word to mankind.

It is our fervent hope that through the study of the books the children will be encouraged to read the Scriptures themselves. So many people are taught all about the Scriptures but few are taught to read them. St Jerome tells us that to be ignorant of the Scriptures means to be ignorant of Christ. This point is stressed by our Holy Father in his recent encyclical letter on the Bible. His Holiness explains that our Divine Lord will be better known, more ardently loved and more faithfully imitated, in as far as men know and meditate on the sacred Scriptures, and especially the New Testament.

Scripture lessons should teach children not only about the Scriptures, not only about the facts of our Lord's life, but about our Lord Himself. They should be taught to know our Lord through the reading of the New Testament. "Everything in the Scripture," says St Paul, "has been divinely inspired, and has its uses; to instruct us, to expose our errors, to correct our faults, to educate us in holy living" (2 Tim. 3. 16).

May the devout and frequent reading of the Scriptures inspire us to a greater love of our Blessed Lord.

✠ BERNARD CARDINAL GRIFFIN

Archbishop of Westminster

INTRODUCTION

by the General Editor

THE great G. K. Chesterton, whose lightest intuitions were usually so much juster than most men's laborious reasoning, wrote of Macaulay: "His noble, enduring quality in our literature is this: that he truly had an abstract passion for history; a warm, poetic and sincere enthusiasm for great things as such; an ardour and appetite for great books, great battles, great cities, great men. He felt and used names like trumpets." These same high attributes may be discerned in the present admirable work by Fr Dyson and Fr Jones, which provides so clear an introduction to Messianism in the Old and New Testaments. Many of us have been obliged to read, without a shred of ardour or enthusiasm, the books of certain older writers on Old Testament history and theology who were quite unable, despite sincere belief and abundant scholarship, to make their subject either interesting or convincing. For them, it would seem, the analysis of documents, the arrangement of chronological tables, and the preparation of material for context-questions, were all far more important than the ardent monotheism which, coupled with a firm hope in the Messias who was to come, sustained and consoled the people of Israel throughout two thousand years of chequered history.

The joint-authors of this book, enlightened and successful professors as they are, have been careful to put first things first, and to insist, as they tell us in their preface, upon "the profound *unity* of the divine plan for the salvation of our human race." Their work combines two excellences seldom found in each other's company—it is as an outline very complete, yet it does not seek to exhaust the subject or to fetter the imaginations of teachers and taught. It should be assured in advance of a gratifying welcome.

JOHN M. T. BARTON

St Catherine the Martyr, West Drayton,
Holy Innocents' Day, 1946

PREFACE

THIS short book is offered as a simple guide through the Old Testament to the New, in the hope that it will show the profound *unity* of the divine plan for the salvation of our human race. For indeed it is one and the same God who speaks in both Testaments, "in times past to the fathers by the prophets" but "in these days, by His Son" (Heb. 1. 1–2).

Biblical quotations have been for the most part reduced to references; it is for the teacher, therefore, to provide himself with a Bible which may later be supplemented by the one-volume Catholic Commentary now in preparation. The references have in many places been inserted in the text rather than buried alive in footnotes. The historical background has been reduced as far as appeared advisable; the discretion of the teacher may reduce it still further. As for the dates, may we plead that the student's memory be not unnecessarily tortured?

The authors wish to thank the Rev. Geoffrey Cunliffe of Upholland College for his kind help with the maps.

R. A. DYSON, S.J.
A. JONES

Upholland,
Feast of St Thomas Aquinas,
Patron of Catholic Schools, 1945

PREFACE TO THE SECOND EDITION

SINCE the publication of the first edition of this little book the Catholic Commentary referred to in the former Preface has appeared under the title of "A Catholic Commentary on Holy Scripture". This may be usefully consulted.

Since then, also, my great friend Father Robert Dyson has died. The kind reader is asked to pray for his soul.

Like the first, this second Preface is dated, by a happy coincidence:

The Feast of St Thomas Aquinas, 1960

ALEXANDER JONES

CONTENTS

CONTENTS

CHAPTER I

THE KINGDOM AND THE REDEMPTIVE PLAN

I. God's Plan

Sacred Scripture is an inspired account of the plan by which God in His mercy willed to restore to fallen man his lost status as "a son of God" (Jn. 1. 12 f.). It is therefore an epic of the long warfare of God's love with the powers of evil. Had that battle been engaged only between God and Evil, the issue could not have been for one moment in doubt: God's victory would have been complete and instantaneous. But this was not so: the victory would always be God's but the fight was Man's. Now man is a free creature; he could, and did, desert the divine cause. Sacred Scripture is therefore a human history also; it deals with all the unforeseeable events which lie within the free and fickle will of man, now rallying to Good, now deserting it. Sacred Scripture describes how the divine plan fared when it operated through free man. This is what gives the story its interest, but for us it is not an anxious interest because we know the end.

II. Israel's Place in the Plan

The Old Testament, therefore, is history of a special kind: it is redemptive history. It tells us how God, in His generous designs for fallen man, gave to one nation a special mission to perform in the accomplishment of this plan. A Kingdom of God was to be established on earth and this Kingdom was to have a twofold aspect or form of existence: the Kingdom of the Old Covenant and the Kingdom of the New. The Jewish nation was to be identified with the first of these two

I

stages of the Kingdom; the people of Israel were to be a national, and at the same time a religious, unit—the only Kingdom of God on earth. The second phase of the Kingdom was to be different; it was to be born, indeed, from the bosom of Israel and its eternal King was to come of Davidic stock but, being purely spiritual in character, it was to ignore all preference of race and to embrace men of all nationalities. Through the merits of its King full membership of this Kingdom was to restore to man the divine sonship which he had lost by the Fall.

Why was it Israel that God chose? The final answer is God's own secret, but one or two human reasons suggest themselves. In the first place, Israel has always been a people apart with a strong racial sentiment; she would guard a divine revelation jealously as a national possession. Secondly, Israel's land and her cast of mind lay midway between Far East and Far West; it was a suitable place and mentality for receiving a revelation destined ultimately for the whole world. We may also add that Israel's very weakness, compared with mighty neighbours like Egypt and Assyria, would commend her to God because, as St Paul says, he chooses the weak the better to show his own power.

But a more important question is: what does such a choice *mean*? Let us remember first that it does not mean that God did not love all other men. All nations could come to know him sufficiently if they had the good will (Rom. 1. 20 ff.). But what God did for the pagans before the coming of Christ is known only to him and the Old Testament tells us very little about it. We must remember too that the "choice" is rather what we should call a "vocation", a call to do some special work for God; that we have been called to do it is one thing, that we do it well is quite another—and it is on this second that salvation depends. Israel as a whole had a "vocation" and the work was done often despite herself, but we are shocked to find how few Israelites did the work well. We unfortunately cannot judge the whole nation by its inspired religious books, for these were written only by the best in Israel. This consideration leads us to our next point.

III. The "Remnant" of Israel

When thinking of God's "choice" we might imagine the whole of the Bible, Old Testament and New, as a huge letter "X", or if you like as one upright and one inverted cone on top of it, poised tip on tip. The base of the inverted cone figures the entire universe with the story of whose creation the Old Testament opens. From all this universe God chooses out our world and from that world Man (*adam* in Hebrew). When the first man sins God undertakes to save Man from his worse self, and the book of Genesis (looking back over an immeasurable distance of time) shows how He set about it. Of the three named sons of Adam God chooses Seth, because Abel is murdered and Cain is the murderer. Of all the descendants of Seth only the family of the faithful Noe is traced, others if named are dismissed from the narrative. Of Noe's sons, Cham, Japhet and Sem, only Sem is selected for special notice. God, the sacred author wishes to say, chose the Semitic races for His instrument. At this point (and here dateable history begins) Abraham the Semite is "called", and to him the great promises are made. Of Abraham's sons, Isaac and not Ismael (ancestor of the Arabs) engages our author's attention, for Isaac was father of Jacob whose other name was Israel. Thus the scope of God's plan is narrowed down: the divine "choice" falls upon Israel, through her the divine work is to be done.

Through every single Israelite, or even through the majority of Israel? Neither. There is a word that keeps recurring in the Old Testament that we translate "Remnant", "Those who are left". It might have been translated "the Chosen Few". This Remnant, these Few, are those (their number is constantly diminishing) who hold on to God through all temptations and national disasters. After the greatest disaster of all, the Babylonian exile in the sixth century, this Remnant consists of those who returned to a desolate land to build up Jerusalem again and to worship God in all sincerity. All this meant suffering and courage. The ideal Israelite therefore, the Remnant at its very best, was the one who endured for God's cause. We shall see later (p. 82) how a prophet paints this portrait, the portrait of God's Suffering Servant; we shall see also how this portrait came to life perfectly in one, and that one our Lord. He is the apex of the inverted cone we spoke of, the final narrowing down of the "choice", Israel's boast, the divine ideal, the Son of God. In him and from him the "choice" expands again (our upright cone) and he will call the Twelve and the Seventy and the Three Thousand of Pentecost Day, and Paul will go out to the Roman world and his followers to the end of the world, because our Lord said: "Go and teach all nations".

IV. Future Kingdom and King

The Old Testament describes the historical fortunes and function of the chosen people, but it also witnesses to a long period of *expectation*. It is a history of a people more concerned with a Kingdom that will be established in the future and with a King who will come to establish it. This expectation begins with God's first promise to mankind after the Fall, a promise wide in its terms but containing in itself the seed of what was to come. That promise finds repeated and clearer expression through the centuries until we find that a King is to come from Israel who will rule all nations for God, a Prophet who will teach them His Law, a Priest who will offer acceptable sacrifice. It was natural enough that this expected King should come to be called "the Anointed

One",[1] for the king and the high priest in Israel were each anointed in token of the mission and power they received from God; with much greater reason the future King-Priest could receive the title "Anointed" so that it eventually became his title more than any other's.

This was the title which Jesus of Nazareth claimed for Himself, not only in private (Mt. 16. 14–17) but also in present of Israel's constituted judges (Mk. 14. 61). He claimed, therefore, to be the expected King of the expected Kingdom, the goal of Israel's hopes and prophecy. Hence it is clear that, if we are to understand His claim and its meaning, we must examine those hopes and that prophecy. This we shall do against the background of the historical circumstances which make the prophecies intelligible. The introduction of these circumstances will also serve to show how all history led up to the coming of King and Kingdom and how the nations—Egypt, Assyria, Babylon, Persia, Greece, Rome—played their part in the divine scheme. We shall identify the King in the person of Jesus of Nazareth, second Person of the Blessed Trinity who assumed a nature like ours in all save sin, who by His teaching showed man the way to the Father and who by His sacrificial death atoned for sin and "gave to them that believed in Him the power to be the sons of God" (Jn. 1. 12).

[1] Hebrew: Mashiach; Greek form: Messias; Greek translation: Christos. The prophets did not use this title for the future king (except Hab. 3. 13) though it is so used in Ps. 2. 2. It had become usual in our Lord's time (e.g. Jn. 1. 25).

CHAPTER II

THE FOUNDATIONS OF THE KINGDOM

I. THE CREATION AND THE FALL

The first three chapters of the book of Genesis form a prologue to the whole of Biblical history. Their inspired author sets out to answer the fundamental questions: "How did this world come into being?" and "Why is it in need of redemption?". He answers the first by showing that the world itself and man upon it are the work of one and only God. The second question still remained to be answered, and all the more urgently because the writer had already said that the world, as it left the hands of God, was "good". The answer to the second question is the story of the Fall.

The prologue opens on earth, made by God and peopled by Him with living things, highest of whom were the first human creatures. These human beings, too, were made of earth but were also created in their nature "the image and likeness of God". In this, man was above the beasts: he is their master (Gen. 1. 26), God is his. Moreover, in understanding and will he resembles God as the beasts do not. This revelation of human dignity prepares us for, but is greatly surpassed by, the New Testament revelation of the power of supernatural grace by which we become "partakers of the divine nature" (2 Pet. 1. 4).

Man had thus received his place in creation. There remained yet to be accomplished Man's own free acknowledgment and regulation of his relationship to God, for Man was a free creature. Would free Man conform in all things to the order of the universe as outlined by God? Would he thus win for himself the name "good" which had been pronounced over the other works of creation? God imposed one grave command as a test (Gen. 2. 17).

At this critical moment another factor appeared, a factor of disorder; its evil nature betrayed itself in incitements to revolt against the divine ordinance. Adam succumbed and evil entered the world. The effects were instantaneous. Man was driven from the Garden (Gen. 3. 23) to dwell in the common plane of the world (Gen. 3. 19) and so lost the privilege of living on (Gen. 3. 22). This world in which Man now found himself was not docile: dominion over animal life had gone and the soil itself would offer him "thorns and thistles" for his labour (Gen. 3. 18–19). As for the woman, her chief function as man's "helpmate" (Gen. 2. 18) in their common parenthood of the human race had been intended for her crowning joy, but it was henceforth to be her pain (Gen. 3. 16). Reason's control of the lower emotions was gone (Gen. 3. 7, 10). Finally, Man lost the supreme gift of that supernatural life by which, in the present order, he is constituted a friend of God.

We, the offspring of these first human parents, are born deprived of that supernatural life and are unable, therefore, to reach our supernatural destiny. In theological terms, we are born "in original sin". But the New Testament insists that this supernatural life, a sharing in the divine nature, an adoptive sonship of God, though lost to us in Adam has been restored in and by Jesus Christ. Mankind in one man lost it; in one Man mankind won it back. In Christ we are once again more than natural Man. Man is "born again" through Christ and His redeeming work. Man's supernatural life and lost relationship with God is restored.

II. THE PROMISE

Even while pronouncing sentence upon our first parents God showed that the triumph of evil in this Fall was not the

victory it might have been. He punished the sin but encouraged the sinners with a promise of complete victory over
the powers of evil represented by the serpent:

> "I will put enmity between thee and the woman,
>   and between thy seed and her seed.
> He shall crush thy head,
>   and thou shalt wound (or 'lie in wait for') his heel."
>
> (Gen. 3. 15.)[1]

In this text, the following points seem clear. First, God
passes sentence not upon a natural serpent but upon the
power of evil who used either a real serpent or the appearance
of one as his instrument. Second, the "woman" in question
is Eve since she alone appears in the context. Third, the
"seed" of the serpent includes all other evil spirits and
perhaps also human sinners who by transferring their
allegiance become rather the offspring of Satan than the
sons of God. Fourth, the "seed" of the woman Eve is
humankind, for she is "the mother of all the living". Fifth,
while the serpent can do no more than wound (or "set snares
for") the heel of Man, Man will crush the serpent's head—
a deadly blow in the most vulnerable part.[2]

III. Hope through the Semites

It is evident that the author of Genesis intends us to look
to the Semitic peoples for the fulfilment of the divine
promise he has recorded in his third chapter. It is expressly

[1] In certain passages we quote not the Douay Version but an authorita-
tive emended reading.

[2] That one Man was to conquer Satan on behalf of mankind and that
Mary His mother was in God's mind when He announced the coming
victory is clear to us in the light of later revelation. This would not appear
to our first parents from the actual words of the promise. Yet because the
text, in telling us that the vanquished will be one, insinuates at the same
time that the victor will be One, and because in the full realization of
this promise an individual descendant of Eve did crush the serpent's
head, the passage is rightly regarded as the first "good tidings", the
"Proto-evangel", of the Messias and of His saving mission.

said, not of Cain nor even of Abel, that Adam begot a son in his own image and likeness, which was the very image and likeness of God (Gen. 5. 1–3). The son's name was Seth. He in his turn had a son Enos who "began to call upon the name of the Lord", (Gen 4. 26), and of him was descended Henoch who "walked with God" just as Adam, it seems, had once "walked" (cf. Gen. 3. 8 and 5. 24). It is in the descendants of Seth, then, that the hope must lie. Yet even of these descendants most were perverted "and the wickedness of men was great on the earth" (Gen. 6. 5). One alone was worthy: Noe. With him alone and his family we are left by the author who sweeps all others away by the Deluge (Gen. 6–8). It is clearly through him that the promise of Gen. 3. 15 must pass, because the rest of mankind had shown itself unworthy.

Of Noe's three sons, Sem, Cham and Japhet, our attention is fastened upon Sem by reason of the blessing pronounced over him by Noe:

"Blessed be Yahweh, the God of Sem; be Canaan his servant,[1]
May God enlarge Japhet and may he dwell in the tents of
Sem, and Canaan be his servant." (Gen. 9. 26–27.)

The gradation among the sons: master, guest, slave, turns the reader towards the family of Sem (Gen. c. 10). Now of this family was Abraham.[2]

IV. ABRAHAM AND THE PROMISES

Abraham, son of Terah, was the founder of the Hebrew nation. His family, a branch of Sem's posterity, was settled

---

[1] Canaan was the son of Cham (Gen. 9. 18).

[2] To carry the reader on from the Deluge to Abraham the sacred author draws up a Table of the Nations and gives a long list of the descendants of Sem. But he also tells a story illustrating how the pride of man (cause of the original Fall) brought disunion among the peoples of the earth (Gen. 11. 1–9). This disunion is typified by a difference of language. The miracle of tongues at Pentecost (Ac. 2. 5–12) indicated that this disunity could be repaired through the Spirit of Christ.

in Ur of the Chaldees in the lower end of the Euphrates
valley. Again there appears a religious division: Terah was
an idolater, he and his sons "served other gods" (Jos. 24. 2),
but Abraham emerges as champion of monotheism. The
family had emigrated to Haran in Mesopotamia where Terah
died. Abraham, then in his seventy-fifth year, migrated by
divine command to the land of Canaan in the company of his
wife Sarai and of Lot, his nephew (Gen. 12. 5). The reason
for the divine command is evident: it was God's plan to
segregate Abraham and his family and to make of them a
people sacred to Himself with a special part to play in the
divine scheme. Abraham's unquestioning obedience (Gen.
12. 4), later to survive the most rigid test (Gen. c. 22),
earned a blessing which marks a significant stage in the
reversal of the sentence passed upon Adam's disobedience.
This blessing took the form of a promise, variously repeated[1]
but essentially complete in its first expression:

"Go forth out of thy country, and from thy kindred, and out of
thy father's house, and come into the land which I shall show thee.
And I will make of thee a great nation, and I will bless thee and
magnify thy name, and thou shalt be blessed. I will bless them that
bless thee and curse them that curse thee, and in thee shall all the
kindred of the earth be blessed." (Gen. 12. 1–3.)

Here Abraham was promised a home for his clan (Canaan,
or Palestine), wide fame and a numerous posterity, the
spiritual and temporal blessings of God; the fortune of other
tribes would depend upon their relations with him and his
descendants. Finally, in the prediction that all nations would
be blessed in Abraham and in his offspring there is foreshadowed a universal salvation which is to be worked
through one people—the stock of Abraham. The promise is
sublime, but its narrow interpretation was to lead to the rigid
nationalism which dominated the later history of Israel.

In other passages connected with the story of Abraham

[1] Gen. 12. 1–3; 15. 1–21; 18. 17–18; 22. 16–18.

God further determined the relationship between Himself and the Abramitic family by making a pact, or "Covenant", with Abraham (Gen. 15. 18; 17. 2). This pact, though in itself an act of pure condescension on the part of God was, in a sense, two-sided since it imposed "obligations" on both contracting parties. Abraham and his posterity were to worship God in a special manner, and God for His part promised to reward them with special blessings, temporal and spiritual. Moreover, all who entered into this Covenant were to bear the mark of circumcision (Gen. 17. 11).

The ancient practice of circumcision which gave a man full membership of his clan thus became a sign of membership of God's chosen people. The circumcised now fully belonged to Abraham's family; he now shared both the privileges and the obligations of the Covenant. Circumcision was an indelible sign of that social-religious bond by which the descendants of Abraham were united with one another and with God. The Covenant made by God with Abraham was a decisive stage in the establishment of God's Kingdom on earth; circumcision associated its recipient with the process of this establishment. Like Baptism it was a rite of initiation into the Kingdom of God, such as the Kingdom then was.

The Covenant with Abraham, therefore, laid the foundations of the Kingdom of God on earth. By this Covenant the Kingdom already had its essential qualities which were: the sovereign rule of God and the corresponding submission of His people; the benefits to be bestowed by God and the obligations to be fulfilled by the people; finally, an external sign identifying and distinguishing all who belonged to the Kingdom. This initial stage of the Kingdom is marked by the change of Abram's name to Abraham.[1] In the later

---

[1] The suggested meaning of Ab-ram ("of noble parentage") is doubtful. Ab-raham is interpreted by the author as "father of a multitude", making the name fit the divine promise.

significant stages of the Kingdom's development the name of Jacob was changed to "Israel" and of Simon to "Peter".

The divine promise was repeated to Abraham's son, Isaac (Gen. 26. 1–5). Isaac's brother, Ismael, though destined to be the ancestor of a numerous people (Gen. 21. 18) was not chosen as the instrument of the divine designs (Gen. 21. 12); the sacred author, in consequence, dismisses him and his descendants in a short genealogy (Gen. 25. 12–18).

By a stratagem not wholly praiseworthy, Jacob son of Isaac had supplanted his brother Esau in the paternal bless-ing and in the rights of the first-born son, though these belonged to Esau as the elder of the twins (Gen. 27. 5–27). It was Jacob who received the divine promise (Gen. 28. 13–16) and Esau, after his family-tree has been described (Gen. c. 36), vanishes from the story.

V. Jacob's Blessing

The third generation of Abraham's family grew into a considerable clan in Canaan but their activity seems to have been limited to pastoral pursuits. They were herdsmen with large flocks and appear to have led an isolated, independent life in frequently moved encampments. Though their land was the natural bridge between Assyria and Egypt, the two most cultured and most powerful nations of antiquity, the Israelites had as yet no art, no literature, no culture, not even a national consciousness. Israel, therefore, was still a child and, as a child, it would have to go to school. The school that God chose for the training of His own nation was, from the cultural point of view, the best procurable—Egypt.

It was Joseph, son of Jacob, who was destined to prepare a place for God's people. Betrayed by his brothers he entered Egypt as a slave but quickly rose to the position of first minister to the pharaoh. At Joseph's invitation Jacob with his entire tribe (sixty-eight men with their children and womenfolk) took up residence in the fertile grazing district of Gessen (Goshen) near Heliopolis. Here they grew into a nation, in fulfilment of God's promise (Gen. 46. 3). Because Jacob's name had been changed to "Israel" (Gen. 32. 24–32) the tribe was henceforth known as "the sons of Israel" or Israelites.[1]

Before his death Jacob blessed his twelve sons, the founders of the twelve tribes of Israel, but Jacob's blessing, like Isaac's, passed over the first-born. Ruben had proved unworthy of the privilege (Gen. 49. 3 f.) and his two brothers next in seniority had forfeited the favour by their inhuman conduct of the war against the Sichemites (Gen. 34. 25–31). Juda, the fourth son, received the blessing of Jacob and with it the promise that from his stock the future King would be born.

The blessing of Juda, like the others in this series, is rich in oriental metaphor and the imagery adds difficulty to a passage which already contains problems connected with the correct reading:

"Juda, thee shall thy brothers praise:
Thy hand shall be on the necks of thy enemies;
Thy father's sons shall bow down before thee.
Juda is a lion's whelp;
From the prey, my son, thou art gone up:
He stooped down, he couched as a lion,
And as a lioness; who shall rouse him?
The sceptre shall not depart from Juda,
Nor the ruler's staff from between his feet,
Till he comes to whom it belongs,
To whom is the obedience of the nations.
Tying his foal to the vine,
And his ass's colt to the choice vine.
He shall wash his robe in wine,

[1] Ya'aqob means literally "he seizes the heel", then "he supplants" (Gen. 25. 25; 27. 36). Yisra'el: "to persevere with God" hence "to win God's blessing" (cf. Gen. 32. 24–32; Os. 12. 3 f.).

> And his garment in the blood of the grape.
> His eyes shall be red with wine,
> And his teeth white with milk."
>
> (Gen. 49. 8–12.)

In the form in which it has come down to us this blessing
of Jacob promises a great king of Juda's tribe ruling over the
nations in a new era of prosperity; it has much in common
with the predictions of Isaias and Micheas (pp. 62, 64).
From Juda sprang the long line of Davidic kings to which
perpetuity was later to be promised (p. 48). St Matthew
traces our Lord's descent from Juda (Mt. 1. 3), and when
St John calls Jesus "the lion of the tribe of Juda" he is
offering an inspired interpretation of our text (Apoc. 5. 5).

Chronological Note

It is plain that the earliest chapters of the book of Genesis
(cc. 1–11) are not meant to be a historical record in the
common sense of the phrase. They tell us that one God
effortlessly created the world, that man, the crown of this
creation, freely betrayed his own high destiny, that murder
and vice followed on the first human sin of pride, that divine
punishment followed. These are necessary theological truths
and they are facts of history, that is to say they actually
happened; but it would be idle to attempt to assign a date to
them. Scientists and anthropologists must be left to deter-
mine, if possible, when the formation of the world took
place and when the first man appeared. These are important
investigations but the story of man's redemption does not
depend upon them and this, after all, is what the Bible claims
to be.

With Abraham, however, we find ourselves in the light of
history in the sense that we are in possession of traditions
concerning his career which reflect the conditions of an age
fairly well known to historians. We therefore begin the

following list with Abraham, but it must be understood that the earlier dates are, naturally, more approximate than the later.

1850 B.C.	Abraham arrives in Canaan (Gen. 12).
1800–1700	Isaac. Jacob (Gen. 25–36).
1700–1600	Joseph in Egypt; followed by the sons of Jacob (Gen. 37–50).
1250–1230	Moses and the Exodus (Ramses II, 1290–1234, being the "pharaoh of the oppression").
1220–1200	Josue invades Canaan. Capture of Jericho.
1200–1030	Judges Period. Conquest of Canaan.
1040–1010	Saul.
1010–970	David. Jerusalem captured, 1000.
970–931	Solomon. Temple built in 968.

CHAPTER III

CONSOLIDATION AND CONQUEST OF THE KINGDOM

I. CONSOLIDATION

I. ISRAEL IN EGYPT

The book of Genesis has now succeeded in focusing our attention upon the clan of Jacob (that is to say, of Israel) which so far consists only of the twelve sons of Jacob with their families. But God had promised to make them into a great nation, a nation that was to be at the same time His Kingdom on earth. We shall now try to outline the steps by which, in fulfilment of the promise, the Kingdom of the Old Testament was formally established.

The majority of historians today place Israel's stay in Egypt from the seventeenth to the thirteenth century before Christ. In this hypothesis, Israel lived under the rule of fellow-Semites, the Hyksos dynasty then in power (about 1720–1560). She prospered in the land of Goshen (Gessen), the pastoral district allotted to her on Egypt's north-eastern border. Centuries later, however, there arose "a new king over Egypt who knew not Joseph" (Exod. 1. 8), a king, that is, who refused to recognize the privileged status of the foreigners from the north. It would seem that this "pharaoh of the oppression" was Ramses II (1301–1234) and that Moses led his people from Egypt either during his reign or in that of his successor Mernephtah (1234–1225), at some date between 1250 and 1230.

The Israelites' fortunes changed. They were conscripted for slave-labour on the new city of Pi-Ramses which was to be the capital of Ramses II (Exod. 1. 11). In these conditions there was little danger that Egyptian contacts would corrupt

Israel's mind: the oppressed do not sympathize with their oppressors; the polytheism and animal-worship of Egypt would have no appeal. Persecution would only draw the Israelites closer together. A common religion and a common sorrow therefore gave birth to a national and religious consciousness. The Kingdom of God was being slowly formed.

II. Moses

For the next step forward in the accomplishment of the Redemptive plan, we turn to the book of Exodus. The purpose of the book will be understood if we keep in mind God's will to redeem mankind by means of a chosen people and eventually by One from among that people. The book of Genesis has traced this design from the beginning of the world down to the separation of the families of Abraham, Isaac and Jacob; it has brought the privileged race from Mesopotamia, through Syria and Canaan and to its temporary settlement in Egypt. The book of Exodus now takes up the story. The small chosen family is now a great people with a national consciousness; it goes forward confidently to receive its Land and its Law.

Moses is the central figure of the book for he was the divinely chosen liberator, the spokesman of God and the instrument of His Covenant. He was of the tribe of Levi, born at the time when the pharaoh had decreed the drowning of every new male child among the Israelites (Ex. 1. 22). The "goodly child" Moses, after three months' concealment, was exposed in a basket on the banks of the Nile (Ex. 2. 5). His elder sister, Miriam, induced the pharaoh's daughter who had rescued the child to entrust him to a Hebrew nurse. The nurse was the child's own mother, Jochabed, who "when her son had grown up" (Ex. 2. 9) delivered him to the princess. In his new surroundings Moses was schooled "in all the wisdom of the Egyptians" (Ac. 7. 22) and next appeared as a sturdy champion of his kinsfolk (Ex. 2. 11 f.). He was forced to flee to Midian, in the Sinaitic peninsula, where an act of rustic gallantry secured him a home with Raguel Jethro, the priest. Sephora, one of Raguel's daughters, eventually became his wife and Gersam his first-born (Ex. 2. 11–22).

After forty years of shepherd life he was chosen by the one God who had pursued His plan through Abraham, Isaac and Jacob, to deliver his people from Egypt. He was to conduct them to Canaan, the land long since promised to the offspring of Abraham. At the same time God revealed the form of the name by which He wished to be known in Israel: "Yahweh" (Ex. 3. 14–15).[1] With Aaron his brother, Moses now returned to his compatriots in Egypt. Their reception among their own people was encouraging and the brothers approached the pharaoh with a preliminary request (Ex. 5. 3) which he unwisely refused. The ten plagues (Ex. cc. 7–12) convinced even the professional magicians. The pharaoh wavered but did not yield. The tenth plague, however, was decisive. Forewarned by Moses, the Israelites prepared to leave the country at a moment's notice and celebrated the first "Pasch", or "Passover",[2] equipped for the journey. The

[1] In Hebrew the sacred and personal name of God is written with the four consonants: YHWH (or, less suitably, JHVH); its original pronunciation was probably YAHWEH. The loss of the certain tradition of pronunciation is accountable to the later Jews who, from motives of reverence, hesitated to pronounce the Name but used its consonants with the vowels of the word "ADONAI" (Lord), to indicate that Adonai and not Yahweh was to be read. These vowels with JHVH would give us approximately JEHOVAH, a word which never in fact existed; its use today proceeds from a misunderstanding of Jewish intentions. The word YAHWEH is part of the verb "to be" and suggests that God's nature is infinitely above man's understanding, i.e., God's answer to Moses is almost "I am who I am". But it is noteworthy that while the false gods are defined in concrete terms (Baal of Fertility, Baal of the Storm, etc.) the true God can only be described, if described at all, in terms of "being"—a notion later to be developed by philosophers and theologians.

[2] The word "Pasch" means "passing over", "springing over"; the Destroyer "skipped" the Israelite houses (Exod. 12. 27).

journey took place on the same day. The first-born of the Egyptians, man and beast, were destroyed by the hand of God and the pharaoh begged the Israelites to leave the country.

The Hebrews who had been the slaves of the pharaoh had been released from that slavery by the act of Yahweh. God, therefore, now acquired a new right over His people. The day of deliverance was the birthday of Israel as a nation, and because it was God who had worked the deliverance the new nation was God's nation.[1] This momentous divine event would always be urged as the motive for Israel's submission, hence the Decalogue begins (Ex. 20. 2):

I am Yahweh, thy God, who brought thee out of the land of Egypt.

Hence, too, the liberation would be called to mind by future generations in the annual celebration of the Pasch (Ex. 12. 14, 42; 13, 1–10).

III. Moses and the Exodus

Avoiding the direct route out of Egypt, blocked by the frontier forts, Moses led his people through the desert. The way was pointed by an advancing column of alternating fire and cloud (Ex. 13. 21). They gained the peninsula of Sinai by crossing the Red Sea. The dry passage, miraculously opened for the Israelites at a point to-day unknown,[2] proved to be

---

[1] Cf. Ex. 6. 6–7; Ps. 113. 1 f.

[2] The uncertainty is inevitable since the whole outline of land and water has been altered by natural changes and by the cutting of the Suez canal. There are two principal theories: (a) The crossing took place at the head of the Red Sea itself, a little north or south of the present Suez; in either place there is shoal water which might have afforded a passage in the circumstances described. (b) The crossing took place some miles farther north, near the Bitter Lakes; this view is now more commonly adopted. In no case does it seem necessary to suppose that the crossing took place in deep sea-water, indeed it would even appear that the contrary is indicated by the sacred text which attributes the division of the waters to a providential "strong and burning wind blowing all the night" (Ex. 14. 21).

a fatal trap for a body of Egyptian pursuers despatched by the pharaoh (Ex. 14. 21–31). The event furnished the theme of the magnificent Canticle of Moses (Ex. c. 15) and made a lasting impression on the national consciousness of Israel.[1]

The journey to the Promised Land had begun. Little guessing how long and how tedious the journey was to be, Israel reached Mt Sinai. Sinai was to live in the memory of the nation for it became the scene of a new advance in the history of the chosen people and therefore in the progress of the divine plan for mankind's restoration. The pact of Abraham's day was at Sinai renewed and reinforced (Ex. 19. 4–8): on the part of Israel worship of the one true God and observance of His precepts, on the part of God a promise that Israel would be regarded as His special possession, as "a priestly kingdom and a holy nation". And the people answered: "All that the Lord hath spoken we will do."

For three days the people prepared themselves by religious observance for the solemn acknowledgment of the Covenant. On the summit of Mt Sinai, Moses received God's conditions of alliance expressed in the Decalogue (Ex. 20. 1–17) and in the civil laws which Moses inscribed in the Book of the Covenant (Ex. cc. 21–23).[2]

On his return, Moses announced to the people all the divine precepts which he had heard on the mountain. On the following morning the whole nation dedicated itself to Yahweh with the most solemn rites that desert conditions would allow:

---

[1] Cf. 1 Kg. 4. 8; 2 Kg. 7. 23; 2 Esd. 9. 10; Ps. 73. 12–15; 76. 15–21, etc.

[2] The laws to be observed by Israel are written in two codices. One of these (Ex. 20. 1–17; cf. Deut. 5. 6–21) contains ten short precepts, the Decalogue. The other (Ex. 21.1 – 23.19) comprises various laws and is known as the Book of the Covenant (Ex. 24. 7). The Decalogue is concerned with religion and morality, the Book of the Covenant chiefly with civil law. The former is unchangeable; the latter, of secondary importance, was subject to change as time and circumstances demanded. Chapters 12–26 of Deuteronomy are its further amplification and modification.

"And rising in the morning he (Moses) built an altar at the foot of the mount, and twelve memorial stones according to the twelve tribes of Israel. And he sent young men of the children of Israel: and they offered holocausts and sacrificed pacific victims of calves to Yahweh. Then Moses took half of the blood and put it into bowls: and the rest he poured upon the altar. And taking the book of the covenant,[1] he read it in the hearing of the people, and they said: All things that Yahweh hath spoken we will do. We will be obedient. And he took the blood and sprinkled it upon the people and he said: This is the blood of the covenant which Yahweh hath made with you concerning all these words."[2] (Ex. 24. 4–8.)

IV. THE CHARTER OF THE KINGDOM

The Book of the Covenant, together with its later and fuller statement in the books of Leviticus and Deuteronomy, formed the written constitution of the Kingdom of God on earth. By this charter the Kingdom of God was formally established. Since God inspired its laws,[3] He was the supreme Legislator, and Monarch of a chosen people; for the same reason there was no sharp distinction between religious and civil laws because all were an expression of the will of Yahweh the King. Israel was a "theocracy", a kingdom

---

[1] In which he had written "all the words of God" (Ex. 24. 4).

[2] The new Covenant was similarly instituted, this time with the much more precious blood of Christ (1 Pet. 1. 19; Heb. 9. 12 f.) who said: "This is My blood of the new covenant" (Mt. 26. 28). It is interesting to notice that twelve men of Israel surrounded the table at the Last Supper just as the twelve memorial stones had stood near the altar of Moses.

[3] This does not mean to say that all the elements of the Law were entirely unknown to Moses or to his fellow Israelites before they came to Sinai, but it does mean that laws and rites traditionally observed and practised are now assumed into the sacred code of the Law and become divine commands. Actually certain practices dated back to patriarchal days (circumcision and sabbath, for instance) and certain adornments of the external religious worship seem to be borrowed from Egyptian art. The Code of Hammurabi (true founder of the Babylonian monarchy, about 1700 B.C.) has many points in common with the Mosaic Law which was formulated five hundred years later. Note that Hammurabi's Code too was chiselled in stone; discovered in 1901–1902 it is to be seen in the Louvre, Paris.

ruled by God, though this rule could and would be exercised through human instruments. These delegates of God were the prophets, the priests and, later, the kings.

The "right of the king" (1 Kg. 8. 11) is described and declared in the book of Deuteronomy (17. 14 f.). He is to rule in the name of Yahweh; God retains His kingship, the human king equally with his subjects is bound to serve Him. It follows that the royal power is limited by the God-given constitution of Israel, that the king is chosen by God as Saul and David were, that he is anointed[1] by a legate of God (a prophet or a priest). If the king did not walk in the way of Yahweh he could be deprived of office. This in fact happened to Saul and to several kings of the northern kingdom. The unfaithful kings of the southern kingdom[2] would have met the same fate had there been no divine promise of perpetuity for the Davidic dynasty.[3]

As for the subjects of this kingdom, they were to constitute a nation separated from all others by distinctive religious beliefs and practices.[4] They were dedicated to the service of Yahweh in love and reverence (Deut. 10. 12). In return for fidelity they were to have peace and fruitful harvests, the blessing of large families, and above all, a particular care on the part of God which is described as His "setting His dwelling-place among them" and "walking with them" (Lev. 26. 3–13). Broken promises would bring famine, plague, war and dispersion among pagan nations (cf. Lev. 26. 14 f.; Deut. 28. 15 f.). Yet God would always be ready to pardon at a sign of repentance and to remember His covenant with His people (Lev. 26. 41 f.; Deut. 28. 64 f.; especially Deut. 30, 1–6).

---

[1] Hence the term "Anointed (Hebrew: Mashiach) of Yahweh".

[2] Ezechias and Josias are the only kings of the dynasty to win unqualified praise (Ecclus. 49. 5 f.).

[3] Cf. 2 Kg. 7. 8 f. David's line rules in Juda until the collapse.

[4] The distinguishing mark of circumcision dates back to patriarchal days; cf. chapter II.

V. TOWARDS THE LAND OF PROMISE

From Sinai the Israelites followed a northerly course towards the Wilderness of Pharan which lies south of Canaan and west of Edom. There they established themselves at Cades (Kadesh Barnea) some fifty miles south of Bersabee (Beersheba). The Bible says very little of the next thirty-eight years but the people evidently led a nomad life in the Badiet-et-Tih (Wilderness of Wanderings) on the southern confines of Canaan. Cades was apparently the centre on which their movements turned. During this obscure period, Israel acquired a greater national solidarity; it developed, too, the ritual and the legislation—both considerably developed under divine guidance—which are described in the books of Leviticus and Deuteronomy.

In the beginning of the fortieth year the march towards Canaan was resumed, but this time it was determined to avoid the difficult southern frontier and to enter the Promised Land by crossing the Jordan at the northern end of the Dead Sea. Passage through Edom and Moab was refused by the king of Edom and the Israelites turned southward towards the gulf of Akabah. Once more on a northerly course, they skirted the eastern frontiers of Edom and Moab, finally encamping by the river Arnon. Resuming their march, the Israelites crossed the Arnon, defeated the Amorrhite chief Sehon and captured Hesebon, his capital (Num. 21. 21–31). In contact now with the northernmost kingdom of Basan, they defeated Og, king of Basan, and occupied his territory (Num. 21. 33–35).

Balac of Moab was alarmed. This new power from the desert, irresistibly advancing, filled him with superstitious fear, and as a true child of his age, he decided to match spirits with spirits. Balac accordingly called in a soothsayer of established reputation, Balaam son of Beor from Pethor by the Euphrates. But Balaam failed him. Under divine

K.P.–C

compulsion the soothsayer who had come to curse remained to bless Israel. In the first three oracles of his blessing, the pagan was forced to proclaim the justice of Israel and God's championship of Israel's cause. In the fourth oracle he had a mysterious addition to make concerning "the latter days":

"I see him, but not now; I behold him, but not near.
A star will come from Jacob; a sceptre will arise from Israel.
It will smite the sides of Moab, and destroy all the sons of Seth.
The land of Edom will be conquered; Seir conquered too.
Israel will fight valiantly; Jacob will rule over its enemies."

(Num. 24. 17–19.)

The pagan seer knows that Israel's advance cannot be withstood, and his oracle evidently concerns the Davidic monarchy. The sceptre is an obvious symbol of kingship and, in the ancient East, the star is also. It was natural that later tradition should apply the star symbol to the royal Son of David divinely promised. Jews and Christians alike saw in it a reference to the ideal, Messianic, king. A Jewish paraphrase of the second century A.D. applies Balaam's words to the Messiah: "And a king will go forth from Jacob and the Messiah from Israel; and he will slay the great ones of Moab and rule over all the sons of men." It is significant too that one leaf of the newly discovered Dead Sea Scrolls[1] applies the "star" passage of Balaam to the "Messiah of Aaron", the Messiah-Priest (cf. p. 84). The great Rabbi Aqiba in the second century A.D. attached the title of "star" to the

[1] This leaf is a list of Testimonia, i.e. of Old Testament passages to be used as ancient oracles applying to the present situation, cf. the use of Old Testament quotations in the New. The leaf was discovered in Cave 4. The Scrolls come from various caves in the hills above the north-west shore of the Dead Sea in the neighbourhood of Qumran. They are of varying dates, roughly from the first century B.C. to the first century A.D. and represent the library of the adjacent "monastery" of Qumran occupied by members of a pious Jewish community (Essenes) from about 150 B.C. to 31 B.C., and again from 4 B.C. to A.D. 68. Further south, other discoveries have been made of documents belonging to the period of the second Jewish Revolt (A.D. 132–135), including an autograph letter of Simon Bar-Koseba himself. The first discoveries were made in 1947; explorers and decipherers have not yet finished their work.

pseudo-Messiah, Simon Bar Koseba whose name already suggested "son of the star" (bar kokeba). Early Christian writers like St Justin in the second century applied the symbol to our Lord; St John in his Apocalypse had already spoken of Jesus as "the offspring of David's line, the bright morning star" (Apoc. 22. 16).

VI. Résumé

With the death of Moses on Mt Nebo in sight of the Promised Land (Deut. 34. 1–7) the second act of the Redemptive drama draws to an end. We have seen how, immediately upon the Fall, God held out hopes of recovery and salvation, though the manner in which this salvation was to be wrought remained undefined. It was to come through a child of Woman (Gen. 3. 15) but, by degrees, it becomes clear that salvation comes through the family of Sem (Gen. 9. 26), of Abraham (Gen. 12. 3), of Isaac (Gen. 26. 3–5), of Jacob (Gen. 28. 14), of Juda (Gen. 49. 10). Balaam seems to say that the salvation will be brought by a warlike Israelitic king (Num. 24. 17), though Jacob (Gen. 49. 10) has spoken of the peaceful aspect of this king's reign, while Moses presents him as a prophet like himself (Deut. 18. 15). We have seen, too, the establishment of the kingdom to which the king will one day succeed (cf. Gen. cc. 12–17; Ex. cc. 19–23) and have heard the promise of the land over which his predecessors were to reign. The Israelites now move forward to possess the land.

II. CONQUEST

I. The Book of Josue

Shortly after the death of Moses, his successor in the command, Josue, resolved under divine guidance to attempt the conquest of Canaan, the country west of Jordan. The story of that undertaking is told in the book of Josue which falls naturally into two parts: the invasion and conquest (cc. 1–12) and the allotment of the land to the several tribes of Israel (cc. 13–24).

The task was not without difficulty. The heights on the western side of the river were crowned with towns, strongly walled and promising stout resistance. With God's special help Josue crossed the Jordan (c. 4) at the head of all the tribes. He pitched his camp at Galgal, four miles from the river, and thence advanced on Jericho. This key to Canaan fell into his hands by divine intervention (c. 6) and Josue marched against Hai, a town two miles east of Bethel, capturing it by stratagem (c. 8). After this rapid conquest of central Canaan, Josue made an alliance with the nearby Gabaonites who had escaped invasion by outwitting him (c. 9). The southern part of the country lay in his power after the battle of Beth-horon and the defeat of a coalition of five Amorrhite kings in that district (c. 10).

Meanwhile the kings of the north had rallied round Jabin, king of Asor in Galilee, and mustered their army near the Waters of Merom (Lake Huleh). Josue surprised and defeated them and proceeded to the conquest of many northern towns (c. 11). Israel had secured a firm foothold in Canaan and the various tribes were accordingly settled in their allotted districts. But it is clear enough from the book of Josue that the Israelites failed to complete the subjugation of Palestine. Many of the larger towns together with cultivated plains and the coast-land remained for a long time in the possession of the Canaanites whose neighbourhood brought disastrous effects on the worship of Yahweh in Israel. The book closes with the death of Josue.

II. THE BOOK OF JUDGES

The personality and generalship of Josue had succeeded in preserving some form of central authority and the Kingdom of God had thrived, for "Israel served Yahweh all the days of Josue" (Jos. 24. 31). With Josue's death things changed. The settlement of the tribes in their various districts loosened the bonds of the old tribal organization, the nation lost its crusading spirit in the comforts and pursuits of civilized conditions, compromise and inter-marriage with the idolatrous Canaanite sapped the strength of Yahwism.[1] National and religious unity had been the secret of Israel's power, its loss brought military misfortune at the hands of the Ammonites, the Midianites, the Philistines, the Canaanites themselves.

Yet something remained of the old spirit which, from time to time, awoke to the appeal of an imposing clan chief. These military leaders, or "Judges", enjoyed also a civil authority which they exercised in accordance with the Mosaic Law, though this authority never extended over the whole land. But the Kingdom of God was in a sad state: the divine scourge of misfortune had brought no lasting cure to its idolatrous frenzies. The book of Judges closes[2] on a sombre note: Samson, one of the last of the Judges, dies in the hands of the Philistines, most dangerous among the enemies of Israel.[3] It was left to Samuel, the last of the Judges, to end the Philistinian oppression (cf. 1 Kg. cc. 1–7).

[1] The two principal Canaanite gods were Baal and Astarte. Baal (mean-ing, in the Semitic languages, "master", "lord") is the supreme god in the Semitic cults; he represents the power of generation and of destruc-tion; as the Destroyer he is named Moloch. At first represented by a pillar, he was later given a human form. He was thought to welcome human sacrifice, and his altogether immoral worship centred round shrines on hills or artificial mounds ("high places"). Astarte, his consort ("queen of heaven"), was represented by wooden columns or trunks of trees standing in the sacred groves by the side of Baal's altar.

[2] Jg. c. 16. Cc. 17–21 are to be referred to the period immediately following the death of Josue.

[3] The Philistines were natives of the Nile delta, of Phœnician stock. They were already established in Canaan in patriarchal times and Greek and Roman authors called that country by their name—Palestine.

CHAPTER IV
THE PROPHETS OF THE KINGDOM

I. The term "Prophet"

Despite the popular use of the word, the "prophet" in Israel was not merely one who foretold the future. The original meaning of the Hebrew word for "prophet" ("nabi") is disputed, but it certainly does not in itself contain the idea of prediction. It appears to mean either "one who is called" or "one who delivers a message". Nor does the Greek word "prophētēs" mean "one who speaks beforehand" but "one who speaks *in the place of another*". It is this meaning which becomes clear from the passages in the book of Exodus where God says to Moses: "See, I have made thee a god to Pharaoh, and Aaron thy brother shall be thy prophet";[1] a little earlier in the same book: "He shall be thy spokesman unto the people; and it shall come to pass that he shall be to thee a mouth and thou shalt be to him as God".[2] The "prophet", then, is the spokesman or mouthpiece of God; one through whom a divine message is conveyed to man. This message may be concerned with the past, present or future; it would therefore be an unwarranted limitation of the prophetic office to restrict it to the foretelling of the future. "The prophets of God speak what they hear from Him, and the prophet of God is nothing else but the enunciator of the words of God to man".[3]

II. What is required in a Prophet

Since the prophet was the spokesman or ambassador of God to man it is plain that his message was based: (*a*) on a commission from God; and (*b*) on divine revelation.

[1] Ex. 7. 1. [2] Ex. 4. 16. [3] St Augustine: *Commentary on Exodus*, c. 17.

The commission from God.—The prophetic office was directly conferred by God. It was not a privilege belonging to a certain tribe, as was the Levitical priesthood, nor was it attached to a determined family, as was the Davidic kingship. It was due to an individual call from God. Of this, the prophets themselves were convinced (Am. 7. 15; Is. 6. 8, 9; Jer. 1. 7; Ez. 2. 2–5; Zach. 2. 9). They betray this conviction when they accuse the pseudo-prophets of usurping a ministry not given to them by God and of delivering a message that is not from God but from themselves (Jer. 23. 16–22; 28. 15–17). They proved their own divine commission sometimes by miracles (e.g. Is. 38. 7 f.), sometimes by a prediction that was quickly verified (Jer. 22. 18 f.). We do not know of any prophet who quite spontaneously offered himself for his mission, rather the contrary: the mission was imposed upon him as a necessity from which perhaps he strove to withdraw (Ex. 4. 13; Jer. 20. 7–9; Is. 6; Ez. 2. 4–8; 3. 6–8) and which he accepted only because of the divine command.

The divine revelation.—God, having chosen His prophets, inspired them to speak as He wished them to do. A supernatural calling was not enough to make a man into a prophet, he received also a supernatural effect in his mind and in his will by which he became a living instrument of God, a mouthpiece of God to man. This supernatural effect we call "revelation". It was God, then, who put His words into the prophet's mouth (Deut. 18. 18), who revealed His secrets to His servants the prophets (Am. 3. 7), who gave them their visions (Am. 7. 1). If God opened the prophet's mouth, the prophet could not be silent; it was, therefore, not "man's impulse that gave us prophecy: men gave it utterance, but they were men whom God had sanctified, carried away, as they spoke, by the Holy Spirit" (2 Pet. 1. 21).

How did God communicate His message to the prophet? Here we must confess to a certain obscurity, for we are dealing with something in the supernatural order. Certainly since prophecy, considered in the prophet himself, is a gift of *knowledge*, it is plain that not only must there be a divine communication but that the prophet must also be sure that it comes from God and must sufficiently understand what the message means. This he is enabled to do by means of a supernatural light infused by God. This divine enlightening of the prophet's mind constitutes the formal and essential element of prophecy. What we may call the material element in prophecy, that is the message itself, may be given to another than the prophet. Thus, for example, Pharaoh had a dream from God but only Joseph could with certainty affirm its divine origin and its significance (Gen. c. 41).

The divine message itself may be communicated in various ways: by words, by visions and by dreams.

Sometimes God spoke directly to His prophets, as He spoke to Moses from the burning bush (Ex. 3. 4–22), though we are not to conclude that this form of communication was used in all cases where it is written that "the word" of the Lord came to the prophet.

Often God "spoke" by means of a vision of which we can distinguish three kinds in Holy Writ. There is the *external* vision in which the object is perceived by the external senses; thus Moses saw the burning bush. There is the *internal imaginative* vision in which the object is seen by the internal imaginative faculty under the form of an image or symbol. To this class belongs the threat of divine punishment revealed to Amos in three tableaux: locusts, fire, war (Am. c. 7); other examples may be found in Is. c. 6; Ez. c. 1; 37. 1–14 and frequently in the prophecy of Zacharias. The third kind of vision, also internal, is called *intellectual* because the divine message was communicated to the prophet's mind without words and without a mental image. Sometimes all three kinds of vision are combined in one revelation. Thus St Paul on the Damascus road had an external vision of heavenly light, an imaginative vision of Ananias, an intellectual vision in which he learned the will of God (Ac. 9. 3, 12, 7).

Communication of a divine message by *dreams* was not uncommon in the patriarchal age (Gen. cc. 28, 31, 37), and in the time of Moses God promised that He would "speak" in dreams (Num. 12. 6). It is clear that these divinely prompted dreams are not to be confused with natural dreams. During the prophetic period such dreams were rare but we have examples in the Infancy Gospel of the New Testament. The Israelitic people were forbidden to interpret dreams themselves (Deut. 18. 10) but were to seek their interpretation from a legitimate prophet alone.

The prophetic *trance* must also be acknowledged as a Scriptural account of the state in which the prophets sometimes received divine revelations. In these trances the bodily senses were closed to external objects as in deep sleep, but the internal faculties of intellect and will were awakened to the highest state of energy.

III. THE ORIGIN OF PROPHECY

Amongst Israel's neighbours there were men who claimed to deliver messages from their gods; the Old Testament itself tells of the four hundred and fifty "prophets" of the Tyrian Baal (cf. 3 Kg. 18. 19–40, and p. 55). Israel too had her companies of prophets from the earliest days of the monarchy, prophets who, stimulated by music and dancing, would fall into ecstasy (1 Kg. 10. 5–10). We find this institution still surviving in the time of Elias (ninth century). Nevertheless, the great Biblical prophets are of a very different kind. The sobriety of their speech and conduct, the weight of their message, are far removed from the frenzy of the earlier prophetic companies. No doubt their actions are at times extraordinary and striking, but such manifestations are the outcome of the earnest conviction that they are the instruments and conveyers of God's urgent message.

The function of the prophet was fully recognized in

Israel. The book of Deuteronomy deals first with the offices of judge, king, and priest (Deut. 16.8—18.8) and proceeds to that of prophet (18. 9–22). After forbidding to Israel the superstitious practices of soothsaying, fortune-telling and the rest, so common among the neighbouring peoples, it states positively how God will provide for His own people: "The Lord thy God will raise up to thee a prophet. . . . And I will put my words in his mouth; and he shall speak to them all that I shall command him" (Deut. 18. 15, 18). Let the Gentiles have their soothsayers, the privileged people of Israel will consult their God-given prophets![1]

IV. The Work of the Prophets

The prophets were authentic teachers given to Israel by God to keep her faithful to her mission and so prepare the way for the establishment of the Messianic kingdom. In the theocratic (or "God-governed") kingdom of Israel the prophet was the legate of the divine King. He stood, therefore, above the people, the priesthood, even the throne itself. We find the prophet in action whenever and wherever God chose to exercise His rights over Israel, whether in the political, religious or moral sphere.

In the political field the prophets advised, admonished, even dethroned kings, not indeed in an arbitrary fashion but by divine warrant. In both the northern and the southern kingdoms they sought to dissuade the rulers from fratricidal strife and from foreign alliances that meant dangerous contact with the polytheism of the surrounding nations. They were lovers of their country but their love sprang from a

---

[1] The word "prophet" is in the singular but indicates a series, like the singular words "king" (in 17. 14) and "priest" (in 18. 3–5). That prophecy was in fact a permanent institution in Israel, a list of the prophets will show. The text, therefore, though applied to the Messiah (Ac. 3. 22) has its primary reference in the series of prophets of whom the Messiah was last and greatest. For this reason our text may be called "inclusively", but not "exclusively", Messianic.

deeper source than exaggerated nationalism: they realized that Israel was not merely a political unit but was also the Kingdom of God on earth with a unique mission to fulfil in the divine plan. The enemies of Israel were for them the enemies of the Kingdom of God.

Their religious teaching emphasized the relation of God to His people; they insisted on the obligations which flowed from that relation, and the chastisement which would follow their neglect. This was the constant theme of their preaching. It was their work to keep alive the religious faith of Israel, to explain and defend the Mosaic Covenant and to keep the people faithful to it. Their first task, therefore, was to wage a bitter and unrelenting war against the polytheism to which Israel was so prone. At the same time they made strong appeal for a more spiritual form of religion than the mere conventional ritual of sacrifice (Am. 5. 14, 22; Os. 6. 6; Mic. 6. 6–8; Is. 1. 11–17; Jer. 6. 20; 7. 21–23). But they did more, they were concerned also for the future. They were the appointed heralds of the divine purpose for Israel and, through Israel, for the world. The manifestation of salvation in its fullest sense; the coming of God Himself to be the Redeemer of His people; the establishment of His kingdom on earth—these were the sublime truths which they were commissioned to proclaim.

In the moral sphere the prophets severely condemned the oppression of the poor, of widow and orphan (Am. 2. 6; 5. 12; Is. 1. 17–23; 5. 23; 10. 2; Jer. 7. 5; 22. 3; Mic. 2. 2). They bitterly rebuked the avarice and injustice of king and priest (Is. 1. 23; Mic. 3. 11; Jer. 2. 8; 5. 31; 6. 13; 23. 1 f.; Soph. 3. 4). In no uncertain terms they denounced the pride and luxury of the people at large (Is. 3. 16; Am. c. 6, etc.).

V. THE PROPHETIC WRITINGS AND STYLE

The greater part of the prophetic books are, in all probability, a condensed report of the spoken prophecies. This seems evident from their brevity and their style: from their brevity, because they are compressed and compact in thought; from their style for it displays an art not common in extempore speech. Indeed some of the prophecies, especially those which were directed to Israelites of the future, may never have been delivered orally at all.

In style there is naturally much difference among the writings of different authors in varying periods. Some books, or portions of books, are in ordinary prose, Aggeus, for example, and Jonas,[1] much of Jeremias, the last section of Ezechiel[2] and parts of Isaias, Osee, Amos and Zacharias. Others are poems with the kind of metrical structure which we notice in the Psalms (thus Joel, Abdias, Micheas, Nahum, Habacuc, Sophonias and Malachy).

To appreciate Hebrew poetry we must understand something of its structure. It is essentially based on *"parallelism"*, that is, on the balance of couplets (occasionally triplets or quatrains) of moderate length expressing or developing the one idea. This parallelism is called *synonymous* when the second line merely echoes the first line with some slight modification (e.g. Ps. 69. 2); *antithetic* when its form is in sharp contrast with that of the first line (e.g. Ps. 19. 8, 9); *synthetic* when the idea expressed in the first line is progressively developed and completed in the following lines (e.g. Ps. 18. 8–10). The line itself is not governed by a fixed number of long and short syllables but by a determined number of stresses or accents; if there are as many as five of these accents, there is regularly a cæsura or pause between the third and fourth.

The prophetic style of writing is figurative and sublime; the form is determined by the age, conditions of life and environment in which the author lived. The Holy Spirit poured His revelation into the mould of these oriental minds; the substance of that divine revelation remains un-

---

[1] Except c. 2.   [2] Ez. cc. 40–48.

changed and without error but its shapes are various. Thus in the prophetic writings we find allegory, parable, symbolic images, strange dramatic actions described, all bearing a marked individuality of style and thought.

VI. THE LANGUAGE OF THE PROPHETS

All who have read the prophetic books agree that they are in great part obscure. Indeed, it would be strange if it were otherwise; books which are over twenty-five centuries old are sure to contain allusions to persons, places, events and customs of which we know little or nothing. But there is a further obscurity which belongs to the passages in which the prophets predict future events. This obscurity existed for the contemporaries of the prophet, even, as it seems, for the prophet himself. It is here that we have the advantage who live after the fulfilment of all that the prophets had obscurely foretold.

The chief reason of this second obscurity is that the prophetic predictions are not a detailed story of future events but merely their foreshadowing. Consequently, the prophets say only as much as is required to prove, after the event had happened, that it had been foretold. The prophets conscientiously passed on the divine message; if that message had not the fullness of Christ's own life and teaching,[1] if their perception of its complete significance was not perfect, they could do no more; they gave what they received. It follows that if God did not choose to reveal the exact date of the prophesied event, the faithful prophet must content himself with pointing vaguely to the future. Often, indeed, we get the impression that the future of which the prophet speaks is to follow almost immediately on present events. The picture is without perspective like the landscape drawing of a child or like a view of distant mountains. At first sight

[1] Heb. 1. 1–2.

this would seem a defect, but closer consideration shows that it is not. A more mature study of history convinces us that dates are of no importance for their own sake, but it is of the greatest importance to know how one event leads up to another, to see the chain of cause and effect through the years. In the eternal redemptive plan of God the time-element is secondary—it is more important to know the "what" than to know the "when". Consequently the prophet Isaias, for example,[1] could connect the Messianic deliverance with the Assyrian invasion. It mattered little whether the enemy happened to be Egypt or Assyria or Babylon, all enemies of Israel were enemies of the Kingdom of God and as such would certainly be destroyed, otherwise there would be no kingdom left for the promised King. *For the sake of* the Messias, therefore, the enemies of the Kingdom would fall[2] as *by* him, in person, their successors (or rather their spiritual instigators) would be scattered. Sacred history revolved, as it were, round the Messias who was therefore equidistant from any point on the circumference.

Finally, the revelation which the prophets received was fragmentary. For the individual prophet the veil of the future was only partially lifted. Each prophecy was, so to speak, a stone in the mosaic; only when those stones were fitted together was the picture recognizable.

VII. THE PROPHETS AND REDEMPTIVE HISTORY

The prophets looked upon history with the eye of faith. They rightly saw that God's hand is upon all the events of this world. They saw that hand especially in Israel's history, because they knew that it was through Israel that God intended to save the world. God was, so to speak, bent on

---

[1] Is. 10.33—11.16.
[2] In Is. 8. 10 the plans of the enemies will be thwarted "because (of) Emmanuel (God with us)".

capturing the world, and Israel was his bridgehead. Now since the one divine mind was behind the whole campaign it was to be expected that the strategy would be consistent and that the operations would all follow the same plan. Thus, to take only one example, there is a repeated pattern of suffering which, humbly accepted from God, always brought men nearer to Him as it always does and always will. Moses and Jeremias, for instance, suffered for their people and thus prepared the most humble of them to see suffering as a weapon of God. When this lesson was thoroughly learned, the colours were already mixed for the great portrait of God's heroic "Suffering Servant" which we find painted in the book of Isaias (cf. pp. 81–83) and in the end brought to life on the Cross. The Cross should not have been a stumbling-block to the Jews, and it was not a stumbling-block to those who had learned God's lesson.

It is the sensitiveness of the great prophets to lessons like these that made the prophets what they were—interpreters of God's ways to man. They had meditated on sacred history and that meditation had been divinely enlightened. They had seen God's work in the past repeated in the present; they were divinely assured that it would be repeated more marvellously in the future. Thus, if God delivered Israel from Egypt, he now delivers her from Babylon and will deliver her (if she will have it) from the greatest empire of all, which is Sin. It was through, and in terms of the events and persons of Israel's past and present that the prophets thought and spoke of Israel's glorious future. By divine revelation the prophets saw Christ's day, but they saw it through the haze of the sacred history of the people to whom they spoke. Prophecy was the misty light that gently prepared the eyes of Israel for the brightness of the Daystar when it rose.[1]

---

[1] Cf. 2 Pet. 1. 19.

VIII. THE MESSIANIC PROPHECIES

It is important to remember what we have said when we read what the prophets had spoken concerning the future King and Kingdom.[1] Their predictions are set down in images drawn from the Old Testament whose history, institutions, worship, individual persons, were a rehearsal of the Messianic Kingdom and King directed by the Master of history Himself. The prophets therefore present the Messiah as a King anointed by God and paint him in colours borrowed from David, his ancestor and shadow. The Kingdom, too, takes on the tints of the Davidic kingdom. Jerusalem and Sion are pictured as the centre of the new Kingdom as they were of the old (Is. 2. 1–4); the Gentiles who are to be received into it are said to "flow unto Mount Sion", to be "born in Sion" (Ps. 86. 4 f.) and to find "salvation" there. The enemies of the new Kingdom are given the names of those nations which were hostile to the Davidic kingdom. All this is explained if we bear in mind that the Old Testament was the pattern and preparation of the New. It was natural for the prophets to illustrate the new Kingdom in terms of the old, especially where more definite revelation concerning the new Kingdom had not been granted.

[1] At this point we should again remind ourselves that such prediction is not the main business of the prophet who is a reformer, a remembrancer of the Covenant, rather than a visionary. Nevertheless, threat and promise necessarily enter into such preaching, hence the prophets' not infrequent concern with the future.

CHAPTER V

THE EARLY FORTUNES OF THE KINGDOM, *c.* 1040–721 B.C.

Biblical books to be consulted:
> *Historical:* 1–4 Kings; 1–2 Paralipomenon.
> *Prophetical:* Amos; Osee.
> *Doctrinal:* Psalms.

I. HISTORICAL OUTLINE

The new monarchical regime was the outcome of a need, strongly felt among the twelve tribes, for a unified military command. It was the will of the majority and Samuel bowed to it, though this imitation of the surrounding peoples betrayed some lack of confidence in the one God who by His powerful providence had made of Israel a nation and established His royal rights. Yet in theory at least Yahweh was not to lose His kingship: the human king was to be no more than His visible representative, the man of His choice[1] and His agent on behalf of the divine Law to which the king himself was to be subject.[2] Israel was to remain a theocracy.

SAUL,[3] *c.* 1040—*c.* 1010 B.C.

The divinely designated king was Saul, a Benjaminite of Gabaa, whose consecration by Samuel and subsequent military successes secured him public acclamation at Maspha. But Saul's failure to realize the theocratic ideal held out by Samuel issued in a breach between the king and the seer who forthwith announced the divine rejection. Yahweh's new choice was David the shepherd, son of Isai (Jesse) of

---

[1] Cf. 1 Kg. 9. 15; 16. 1; 2 Kg. 7. 12 f.
[2] Deut. 17. 18 f.
[3] 1 Kg. cc. 1–31; 1 Par. c. 10.

Bethlehem; he was secretly anointed by Samuel. Meanwhile the king, consequent on the break with Samuel, had fallen into a fit of melancholy to cure which David, an accomplished minstrel, was called to court. It was not long, however, before Saul contracted a morbid jealousy of David's military and social gifts and David became for some years a fugitive before the king's enmity. He found refuge ultimately, with a small band of partisans, at Siceleg in Philistinian territory.[1] When Saul died on Mt Gelboe after a decisive defeat at the hands of the Philistines, David hurried to Hebron where the tribe of Juda saluted him king.

DAVID,[2] c. 1010–971 B.C.

During this period of partial kingship which lasted for seven and a half years David was little more than a vassal of the Philistines who now dominated the country from its northern approaches at Esdraelon. After the assassination of Ishbaal, son and successor of Saul, all Israel declared for David. The Philistines took alarm but David, prudently declining open warfare, reduced them first to the defensive and eventually to impotence. When the frontier powers of Moab, Ammon and Edom had been successively made tributary David was free to turn to home affairs.

Hebron being neither central nor strategically strong, David had already provided himself with a new capital by the reduction of the Jebusite stronghold of Sion, thenceforth "the city of David". Deeply conscious of the favours of Yahweh and of his own corresponding obligation to make of Israel a kingdom of God, David had the ark of the alliance[3]

[1] For this period cf. 1 Kg. cc. 18–31.
[2] 2 Kg. c. 1—3 Kg. c. 2; 1 Par. cc. 11–29.
[3] The Ark, visible sign of the Covenant, had been placed at Silo in Josue's time. It remained there until Samuel's day when it was captured by the Philistines but was returned by them *via* Bethshemesh to Cariathiarim where it stayed for seventy or eighty years. The Mosaic tabernacle, however, was still at Gabaon during David's reign but Solomon

brought with great solemnity to Sion, and Jerusalem became
the religious as well as the political centre of Israel. Liturgical
organization absorbed much of David's later activity, though
the actual building of a temple was reserved to Solomon.[1]
He divided the priesthood into twenty-four teams, eighteen of
the family of Eleazar and six of Ithamar, which were to
function in weekly rotation. The Levitical assistants (twenty-
four thousand in number) were similarly grouped into
twenty-four classes of a thousand each; other Levites were to
supervise the sacred chant, others were appointed to the
provincial courts.

Though never achieving even an approximation to the size
of the empires of Egypt, Assyria, Babylon, the kingdom of
Israel realized its greatest territorial expansion under David.
On the coast the Philistines were cowed and the Phœnicians
friendly; to the north the Aramean states, to the east Ammon
and Moab, were tributary; on the south the Amalecites were
dispersed, the Edomites assimilated. David's indirect sphere
of influence was even wider and extended from the Red Sea
to Damascus and beyond to the Euphrates.

David's faults must be judged against their background.
He had only a modicum of the cruelty and sensuality of the
average oriental monarch, and as a figure of the old Dispensation, he must not be condemned for abuse of the
abundant light and grace which the ages before Christ never
knew. As for his virtues, his personal and active devotion to
Yahweh's cause made him the ideal theocratic king and the
prophets willingly lend his name to the Messias of their
hopes.[2]

---

had it stored in one of the upper rooms of the Temple. Saul had offered
sacrifices at Gabaon and it is evident that the law of unity of sanctuary
(Deut. 12. 5–14) was not observed in those still troublous times since
David himself sacrificed on Sion without attempting to abolish the
Gabaonite sanctuary. To this duality there corresponded a double high-
priesthood: Abiathar, of the family of Ithamar and grandson of Heli,
officiated on Sion; Sadoc, of Eleazar's family, functioned at Gabaon.

[1] 2 Kg. 7. 12 f.   [2] E.g. Ez. 34. 23.

SOLOMON,[1] 971–929

The son of David entered into his inheritance with all the gifts likely to sustain and enhance it. Peace at home and abroad left him free for the project nursed by his father and within seven years[2] a stately temple of Yahweh stood on the hill to the north of Sion; its dark innermost sanctuary housed the Ark.

But the temple was not built without expense and the national exchequer, fed by a system of taxation efficient and oppressive, was further drained by the cost of the sumptuous palace which rose now to the south of the temple, and by the extravagance of Solomon's royal state. His successful commercial development was not adequate to meet his expenditure and most, if not all, of the financial burden fell upon the northern tribes who benefited least from the new magnificence of the capital. There were seeds of rebellion here.

In the sphere of religion, too, the once wisest of kings was storing up trouble for Israel. Influenced by his royal harem, in large part pagan, the builder of Yahweh's temple erected sanctuaries in the neighbourhood of Jerusalem to the Canaanite deities Astarte and Moloch. There was no national apostasy as yet but Solomon was setting a dangerous example.

ROBOAM OF JUDA,[3] 929–913
JEROBOAM OF ISRAEL,[4] 929–909

Roboam, son of Solomon, was no diplomat; he disastrously failed to realize that the northern tribes in general and the powerful tribe of Ephraim in particular, all tender from taxation, needed delicate handling. The result was the providential outcome of his father's sins and the punishment

---

[1] 3 Kg. cc. 1–11; 2 Par. cc. 1–9.
[2] The Temple was begun in 968 B.C. and finished in 961 B.C.
[3] 3 Kg. cc. 12–14; 2 Par. cc. 10–12.
[4] 3 Kg. cc. 12–14; 2 Par. c. 13.

of his own obstinacy. Open rebellion under Jeroboam the Ephraimite, successful this time as it had not been under Solomon, subtracted the northern tribes from Davidic allegiance. Juda with part of Benjamin now stood alone.[1]

Politically and religiously the northern kingdom (called "Israel" for its numerical preponderance) was in worse case than Juda. It had no dynastic tradition: that nine dynasties succeeded each other in its two hundred years of existence is evidence of instability and social distress. It was exposed, too, to the dangerous north. Juda, on the other hand, was buffered from without by Israel while, within, the one Davidic dynasty maintained itself until after three and a half centuries the temporal monarchy passed from Juda for ever.

The consciousness of a divinely chosen royal line, the possession of the centre of religious cult, the more intense prophetic activity, all held out for Juda the spiritual prospects which the northern kingdom lacked. And in fact the religious situation in the north grew rapidly worse. Jeroboam, anxious to promote political independence, forbade pilgrimage to Jerusalem, and ignoring the prescribed unity of sanctuary,[2] he favoured the shrines at Dan (in the extreme north of his kingdom) and at Bethel (on the southern border), presenting a golden calf to each.[3] Juda also, despite its advantages, willingly followed Roboam into idolatrous ways.

Retribution for both kingdoms was not slow to follow. In 925, the pharaoh Sesac, founder of a new dynasty no longer favourable to Israel,[4] invaded Juda, sacked Jerusalem and penetrated into the northern kingdom. Sesac's death in the

---

[1] Cf. 3 Kg. 11. 11 f.

[2] The ordinance of Deuteronomy (Deut. 12. 8–9) demanded one sanctuary when political stability should have been reached. This stability had certainly been achieved in Solomon's day.

[3] Probably no more than representations of Yahweh borrowed from Aramean models, but in open defiance of the Mosaic Law (Ex. 20. 23–24) and threatening to undermine a Yahwistic people.

[4] Solomon's chief wife had been daughter of a pharaoh of the preceding dynasty.

following year fortunately made this an isolated incident, but the almost equally disastrous hostility between the kingdoms of Juda and Israel was not an incident, it was a habit—a habit which persisted for fifty years.

JUDA: ASA, JOSAPHAT,[1] 910–849; OMRI, ACHAB,[2] 884–854

The years that followed the death of Roboam saw the growing and damaging interference of Damascus in Palestinian affairs; Damascus waxed fat on the hostility of Juda and Israel.[3]

Juda under Asa (910–870) and Josaphat (870–849) went through a period of moderate material prosperity and of religious reform, though neither Asa nor his son allowed Yahwistic ideals to interfere with his foreign policy. Thus Asa contracted an alliance with Benhadad I of Damascus against his own co-religionists of the northern kingdom while Josaphat brought tainted blood into the Davidic line by marrying his son Joram to Athalia, daughter of Achab and the idolatrous Jezabel. Nevertheless, Josaphat must be numbered among the most pious kings of Juda. He was forced to tolerate the provincial Yahwistic shrines (the "high places"), as Asa had done, but he took very practical measures for the diffusion of a knowledge of the Law.

The combined reigns of Asa and Josaphat witnessed eight kings and four dynasties in Israel. The fourth dynasty, founded by Omri, steadied the northern kingdom and its relations with Juda improved as the threat from Damascus grew. From the religious point of view, however, conditions worsened and under Achab (873–854) Israel suffered the

---

[1] 3 Kg. 15. 9–34; 2 Par. cc. 14–16; 3 Kg. 22. 1–51; 4 Kg. c. 3; 2 Par. cc 17–20.

[2] 3 Kg. 16. 17–28; 3 Kg. 16.29—22.40; 2 Par. c. 18.

[3] In biblical history the most important of the Syrian (Aramean) states. It was a tributary of Israel in David's reign, recovering independence in Solomon's.

official introduction of idolatry. Dominated by his Phœnician wife Achab built a temple to the Tyrian Baal in Samaria, the new capital which Omri had built. Against this State-sponsored idolatry in the north, the whole life of the prophet Elias ("Yahweh is God")[1] was a vigorous protest and he rightly goes down to history as the champion of Yahwism. The task of Elias and his spirit were inherited by his disciple Eliseus[2] who excelled a master in his miracles whom it was impossible to excel in fortitude or significance. It was Eliseus who inspired the revolt against the idolatrous despotism of the Omrid dynasty which had not mended under its two last representatives, Ochozias (854–853) and Joram (853–842).

JUDA: ATHALIA, JOAS,[3] 842–797;
ISRAEL: JEHU, JOACHAZ,[4] 842–798

Jehu, general of Joram of Israel, was anointed king by command of Eliseus and proceeded to the extermination of Achab's family. At Jezrahel Joram was assassinated together with the queen-mother, Jezabel. Ochozias of Juda who, unfortunately for him but not for Juda, happened to be in the neighbourhood, was also murdered.

When the news of the death of her son Ochozias reached Athalia she massacred all his sons with the exception of the rescued baby Joas and assumed complete control in Juda (842–836). True daughter of Jezabel she had brought pressure to bear on her husband Joram of Juda (849–842) to build in Jerusalem itself a sanctuary to Baal; to grace it she now took the ornaments of Yahweh's temple. But she had miscalculated the strength of Yahwism. Smarting under Athalia's despotism, priests and people hailed their new king

---

[1] 3 Kg. cc. 17–21.
[2] 4 Kg. 2.1—8.15; 13. 14–21.
[3] 4 Kg. c. 11; 2 Par. cc. 22–23; 4 Kg. c. 12; 2 Par. c. 24.
[4] 4 Kg. cc. 9–10; 2 Par. 22. 7–9; 4 Kg. 13. 1–9.

Joas, now a boy of seven, and Athalia was murdered outside
the Temple.

Juda under Joas (836–797) and Israel under Jehu (842–
815) enjoyed a religious revival, though in Israel the dangerous sanctuaries remained at Dan and Bethel. But both
kingdoms now began to feel the Syrian pressure. They therefore naturally chose non-intervention when the Assyrian
Salmanasar III reached the gates of Damascus—Jehu even
went so far as to offer him voluntary tribute. Damascus itself
did not fall and after the Assyrian withdrawal its king Hazael
turned on Israel and seized the whole of Transjordania. His
successors penetrated into Cisjordania and all but annihilated
the Israelite army of Joachaz (815–798) while Joas of Juda
hastened to buy them off with Temple treasures.

JUDA: AMASIAS,[1] 797–789; ISRAEL: JOAS,[2] 798–783

Damascus being once more in difficulties, Joas of Israel
improved the occasion by reoccupying the greater part of
Transjordania. He marched then against Juda and sacked
the capital, allowing a humiliated Amasias to remain on the
throne.

JUDA: AZARIAS (OZIAS),[3] 789–738;
ISRAEL: JEROBOAM II,[4] 783–743

A period of economic and military prosperity in both
kingdoms. Jeroboam of Israel pushed his Transjordanian
territory into Ammon and Moab, having recovered all the
districts lost to Damascus. In Juda, Azarias used the new
conditions to advance the cause of Yahweh, but in Israel the
same conditions were leading to the enervating opulence
which it was the mission of the two prophets, Amos and
Osee, to denounce.

But it was the calm before the Assyrian storm.

[1] 4 Kg. c. 14; 2 Par. c. 25.   [2] 4 Kg. 13.9—14.16.
[3] 4 Kg. 15. 1–7; 2 Par. c. 26; cf. Is. cc. 1–6; Am. 1. 1 f.; Os. 1. 1 f.
[4] 4 Kg. 14. 23–29.

DECLINE AND FALL OF THE NORTHERN KINGDOM, 743–721[1]

While Joatham (738–736) and Achaz (736–721) reigned in Juda, the storm broke on the northern kingdom. By 745 the energetic Theglathphalasar III ("Pul"; 745–727) was on the Assyrian throne. He immediately moved westwards against the Aramean states west of the Euphrates. Samaria was ill-equipped for resistance. Conditions were chaotic[2] and the throne unstable: the last six rulers of the kingdom represented five separate dynasties and covered only a score of years (743–724). Zacharias (743) contrived to reign for six months, his murderer, Sellum, for only one. The brief dynasty of Manahem (742–737) was discredited by Assyrian invasion and imposition of indemnity (738) and the anti-Assyrian party deposed his son Phaceia (737–736). Phacee, who succeeded (736–732), pursued an absurd anti-Assyrian policy, condemned by the prophet Osee,[3] and joined the Syrian coalition with Rasin of Damascus at its head. In 734 the coalition declared war on Achaz of Juda who had refused his support. Achaz, against the advice of Isaias, appealed to Assyria. Within a year Theglathphalasar had destroyed Damascus and occupied Galilee and Transjordania whence the inhabitants were deported.

In Samaria the pro-Assyrian faction rose to power and crowned Osee[4] the last king of the northern kingdom (732–724). The new king remained a faithful vassal of Assyria until the death of Theglathphalasar (in 727) when he approached Egypt with a view to alliance. It was the end. Salmanasar V (727–722), successor of Theglathphalasar, secured the person of the king and laid siege to Samaria, his capital. The surrender of the city, after three years (in 721), was received

[1] 4 Kg. 15. 8–31; 17. 1–41.
[2] Cf. Os. 7. 1 f.
[3] Os. 7. 11.
[4] Not the *prophet* Osee!

by Sargon II (722–705), whose predecessor, Salmanasar, had died during the siege.

In place of the many deported from Samaria, Sargon imported Babylonians, Syrians, Arabs who brought their idolatrous worship with them. Nevertheless it appears that a majority in the northern kingdom remained faithful to Yahwism which eventually overcame the imported cults.

II. THE MESSIANIC HOPE
I. THE BOOKS OF "KINGS"

The first two books of Kings are not a mere catalogue of historical events but a demonstration of God's fidelity to His promise. He had assured Abraham[1] and Jacob[2] that kings would come of their race; He had promised to Juda an enduring sceptre.[3] It is therefore David of Juda who is the central figure of the books of Kings and Samuel appears only as the instrument of God's Davidic choice. Saul is introduced as a contrasting figure of rejected infidelity throwing into relief the final choice of David, the man "after God's own heart". Hence the climax of the books is the promise made to David of a lasting dynasty.[4] This promise is the basis of all subsequent prophecies relative to the future King and Liberator who, in authentic Jewish tradition, is henceforth represented as being of Davidic descent and is even called by David's own name.[5] "I will establish thy kingdom for ever": this promise is absolute, but to it there is joined a second, a conditional one of temporal prosperity in return for loyalty to Yahweh's cause. How subsequent events illustrated these promises is the theme of the third and fourth books of Kings: while dynasties crash in the northern kingdom, the Davidic line in Juda has no successor though its prosperity fluctuates with its fidelity.

[1] Gen. 17. 6.   [2] Gen. 35. 11.
[3] Gen. 49. 8 f.   [4] 2 Kg. 7. 11–16.
[5] E.g. Os 3. 5; Jer. 30. 9; Ez. 34. 23.

In view of the absolute divine promise it is patent that any claim to be the prophesied King and Liberator of Israel would have to be supported by evidence of Davidic descent.[1]

II. The Psalms[2]

i. *The Kingdom*

Underlying Israel's hope of a future religious restoration is the fundamental doctrine of Monotheism. At present worshipped by one chosen nation Yahweh nevertheless, since He is the only God, has unlimited rights. These rights, through Israel's effort, must and will come to be universally recognized.

By unique title of creation Yahweh owns the earth with all its peoples (Ps. 23. 1–2). It is He who, holding them in being, keeps vigilant watch over them all (Ps. 65. 7), brings them to their senses by chastisement (Ps. 93. 10), invites all without distinction to receive His instruction (Ps. 48. 2). It is not therefore surprising that Israel, exclusive as it was, should yet see its God as King, by right, of every nation (Ps. 96. 1 f.). To Him every nation is bound in homage (Ps. 2. 10 f.).

But since Yahweh is all-powerful, it follows that His universal rights will be effectively asserted; indeed He will come in person to assert them (Ps. 49. 3, 22), and woe betide those who resist! This divine intervention, its coming certain, the time of its coming still vague, is the "Day of Yahweh" of which the prophets speak. All the kings of the earth will then bow to the just, beneficent, compassionate rule of Yahweh (cf. Ps. 101. 16; 71. 1–4).

Yet this universal outlook does not impair Israel's consciousness of its own privileged status. Israel is the present

---

[1] Hence the genealogies of Mt. c. 1 and Lk. c. 3.

[2] Conveniently inserted here since more than one half of the Psalms are attributed to David. The remainder of the total of 150 are of later and varying dates.

kingdom of Yahweh (Ps. 113. 1–2), it is therefore by means of Israel that Yahweh will extend His kingship. If the Psalms sometimes paint this extension of divine dominion in warlike colours (e.g. Ps. 2. 9) it is not surprising since, for the nations which surrounded Israel, military conquest meant the adoption by the conquered of the conqueror's gods. But we must not be misled by such images. It is not the sword but the prestige of Yahweh's favours to Israel that will initiate this spiritual conquest (Ps. 66. 1–3),[1] and the victory will be finally won not by arms but by the justice and mercy of the Conqueror (Ps. 71. 11 f.). Then, at the end of this strange war, conquerors and conquered on equal terms worship Yahweh in happy unity (Ps. 46. 10) in a kingdom which knows no end (Ps. 144. 13).

In this conception of the part to be played by Israel it is not strange that the earthly capital of the future universal and spiritual kingdom should be represented as Sion, cradle and sanctuary of David's kingship. Those of all nations who come to know Yahweh lose their nationality to gain the citizenship of Sion which is their true mother-city (Ps. 86) and their religious home (Ps. 95. 7–9). Not even the destruction of Jerusalem nor the dark days of exile could destroy that hope (Ps. 125).[2]

ii. *The King*

The foundation of "royal messianism" is to be found in the prophecy of Nathan (2 Kg. 7. 11–16; cf. p. 48). In Psalm 88 this promise is poetically developed, and the psalmist begs God to remember it at a time when He seems to have "cast off His anointed", that is to say, to have rejected the Davidic dynasty. The same promise is recalled with

---

[1] Ps. 66. 3: read "that *men*" (not "*we*") "may know Thy way upon earth".

[2] Ps. 125. 1 is perhaps better translated: "When Yahweh shall have restored the destiny of Sion we shall be as those in a dream" (i.e. dazed with happiness). The Psalm belongs to the Exilic period.

great confidence in Psalm 131. The idea of God's kingdom seems to have become inseparable from the expectation of a Davidic king.

It is against this background that we have to read Psalm 2. Here the Davidic king, "the Anointed" (Mashiach, Christos) is represented with Yahweh at his side. Against both the unbelieving peoples are ranged, but over these the victorious Anointed establishes his dominion. Yet the end of the war is death and destruction only for those who refuse the law of Yahweh and the yoke of His Christ. The divine edict to this effect is promulgated by the Anointed from Sion, the centre of his kingdom.

Balancing this warlike Psalm is a Psalm (71) of peaceful rule in an acquired empire. The king is not of Palestine only but of the whole earth (vv. 5–11) and all nature joins in the new happiness (vv. 3, 16), a sure sign that the inspired poet is speaking of a future ideal age.[1] The rule of this peaceful king is characterized, like that of the Isaian Messianic king,[2] by particular care for the poor and wretched. Through this king the blessing of Abraham passes to the whole world (Ps. 71. 17; cf. Gen. 12. 3).

It is not surprising that our Lord, promised the throne of David his father (Lk. 1. 32 f.), hailed as David's son (Mk. 10. 47), himself claiming to be a king (Jn. 18. 37), should be looked upon by the New Testament as the fulfilment of the psalmist's prayer, the proof that the ancient promise had not failed. Thus in the Acts of the Apostles (4. 25 ff.) the early Christians take comfort in persecution from the words of Psalm 2: the princes of the earth had indeed risen against God's Anointed, but victory was promised; the enemies of the Davidic king would be his footstool in the end (Ps. 109. 1; cf. Ac. 2. 34 f.).

Towards this chosen dynasty of David God had promised

[1] Cf., for example, the prophetic passages in Is. 32. 15; 45. 8; Ps. 84. 12.
[2] Is. 11. 4; 25. 4; 61. 1.

to act as an affectionate father: "I will be his father, he shall
be my son" (2 Kg. 7. 14). In Psalm 2 the royal prerogatives
of the "Anointed" are the consequence of this sonship
(vv. 7–8). Now it was not uncommon in the ancient East that
the king should be credited with divine sonship, but here the
terms are very emphatic indeed:

> "Thou art My son, this day have I begotten thee."

There is the closest relationship between Yahweh and the
Davidic king. This relationship is even more heavily under-
lined in the Septuagint[1] translation of Psalm 109:

> From the womb before the daystar (was made) I begat thee·

Though the sentence differs considerably from the Hebrew
text, it at least bears witness to a current of Jewish Messianic
thought in the second century before Christ. The Hebrew
text does not speak directly of the divine sonship, but its
phrase: "Thy birth is as a dew" recalls the king of Psalm
71. 6 who, like Yahweh himself,[2] or like His fruitful "word"[3],
descends to earth from Heaven.

The idea of sonship was rich in possibilities. A Davidic
king whose kingdom was not of this world was to enjoy a
sonship which was not simply that of a reigning Davidic
monarch. The Epistle to the Hebrews seizes upon the theme
and shows how, in our Lord's case, this sonship set him above
the angels (Heb. 1. 5), and Christian tradition applies
Psalm 2. 7 and 109. 3 to the eternal generation of the Second
Person of the Blessed Trinity.

Of the Psalms that are called "messianic" the most
frequently quoted in the New Testament is Psalm 109. Its
scene is laid in Heaven. The Davidic king is invited to take
the place of honour at God's right hand. As in Psalm 2, this

---

[1] From Hebrew to Greek, third to second century B.C. St Jerome (in
A.D. 386) revised the existing Latin version of the Psalms with the help
of the Greek Septuagint. This revision is found in the Church's official
Latin version (the "Vulgate") and from it our Douay translation was made.
[2] Os. 6, 3.   [3] Is. 55. 10 f,

king rules widely from Sion, but a new note is struck: the priestly character of the king. The priesthood is not a Levitical one, deriving from the Mosaic Law; it is "after the manner of Melchisedech", the king of Abraham's time upon whom was conferred a pre-Mosaic priesthood by personal and direct act of Yahweh (Gen. 14. 18–20).

In the New Testament our Lord applies the Psalm to the expected Messiah (Mt. 22. 44) and claims for himself the royal honour it describes (Mt 27. 11) and the universal power it speaks of (Mt. 28. 18). But the Epistle to the Hebrews takes up the Psalm's association of kingship with priesthood. Knowing Jesus for the one great mediator between God and man, it adopts the Psalmist's phrase: "a priest after the manner of Melchisedech"; our Lord is no less a priest for having sprung from Juda and not from Levi, indeed his priesthood is so much the greater since it is conferred on him uniquely and not as one member of a priestly family (cf. Heb. cc. 5–9). Later Christian tradition further calls attention to Melchisedech's action in "bringing forth" bread and wine for Abraham (Gen. 14. 18); it sees in this a foreshadowing of the bread and wine of the Holy Eucharist offered to all the spiritual sons of Abraham by the priest-king Jesus.

III. Amos

Born in Juda, Amos exercised his ministry for the most part in the northern kingdom. Fundamental for him is the truth that Yahweh, lord of all nations by right of creation, is in particular King and Father of all Israel by reason of His own free choice. To this choice corresponds the nation's obligation to acknowledge His dominion. In this, the nation had failed. The prosperity of the northern kingdom under Jeroboam II (783–743) had led to social vices and to idolatrous worship in the shrines which had been substituted for the legitimate sanctuary in Juda. Amos therefore predicts

heavy chastisement on "the Day of Yahweh" for all the
nation, not excluding the southern kingdom (Am. 2. 4–5;
6. 1). But he sees "a remnant of Joseph" (i.e. of the northern
kingdom) as the eventual object of divine pity and of
restoration. This restoration will see a revival of the Davidic
dynasty of which the prophet foresees the imminent collapse
(Am. 9. 8–14). Amos, who regards the political split of the
kingdom under its aspect of religious schism, thinks primarily
of a religious restoration and reunion. The last verses of his
prophecy announce the benefits of these happier days in the
characteristically Messianic metaphor of marvellous fertility
of the soil—such fertility as suggests the reversal of Adam's
curse (Gen. 3. 18).

IV. Osee

A native of the northern kingdom and contemporary of
Amos. Immorality, idolatry, ignorance, internal strife are
working the ruin of his motherland to which he appeals as
to the now unfaithful spouse of Yahweh, affianced to Him
since He brought her from Egypt. In view of that sacred
bond Israel must accept no treaty with idolatrous Egypt or
Assyria. The chastisement of her present infidelity will
surely come (it came from the Assyrians), but it will not end
in annihilation, there will be a restoration (Os. 2. 16 f.;
3. 1 f., etc.). Since the northern dynasty is of schismatic
origin the restoration will involve reunion with the house of
David:

"The Children of Israel (i.e. the northern kingdom) . . . shall
seek Yahweh their God and David their king." (Os. 3. 5.)

This will come about "in the last days" (i.e. in the Messianic
age). Osee ends, like Amos, with a description of the era to
come in grandiose agricultural terms.

CHAPTER VI
THE KINGDOM IN JUDA,
736–608 B.C.

Biblical books to be consulted:

Historical: 4 Kings, cc. 16–23; 2 Paralipomenon, cc. 28–35; Judith.

Prophetical: Isaias, cc. 1–35; Micheas; Nahum; Sophonias; Habacuc.

With Samaria shortly to become an Assyrian province,[1] Juda was about to receive a new and uncomfortable neighbour whose influence was to overshadow her story for a century. The restlessness of Egypt and Babylon under the Assyrian empire would aggravate an already delicate situation. If Juda were to prosper, she must walk warily in this new world.

ACHAZ, 736–721[2]

Until the day of his death Achaz lived in uninterrupted vassalage to Assyria. His refusal to join the Syro-Ephraimitic coalition[3] had led to defeat at the hands of Rasin and of Phacee, and he made urgent appeal to Assyria. *Isaias*, whose prophetic ministry had opened in 738, vehemently opposed a policy which betrayed a lack of trust in Yahweh. God Himself could see to the frustration of Juda's present enemies. The policy of Achaz threatened to open the door to Assyria, with all its gods, as a policy of strict neutrality would not have done. But Isaias pleaded in vain with his polytheistic king. His worst fears were realized: subservience to Assyria soon induced Achaz to set up an Assyrian altar in the Temple; about this time, too, (732) he

---

[1] See preceding chapter.
[2] 4 Kg. 16. 1–20; 2 Par. 28. 1–27.
[3] See preceding chapter.

introduced the Assyrian cults of Sun, Moon and Stars. Small wonder that Isaias protests so bitterly against the prevailing idolatry![1]

EZECHIAS, 721–693[2]

Under the influence of the prophet Isaias and of his contemporary, Micheas, the new king undertook the much needed religious reform. The Temple was purified and re-dedicated, the "high places" (provincial shrines which threatened the unity and purity of Yahwism) were removed. There was a movement also towards religious reunion with the faithful of the northern kingdom—a movement which promised to draw spiritual prosperity from material disaster. In the period of peace, Ezechias found time to look to the fortifications and vital water-supply of the capital.

Eventually, however, Juda allowed herself to be caught in the web of international politics. Ezechias, prompted by Isaias, had for the first ten years of his reign resisted the advances of an Egypt bent on the destruction of Assyria, but in 712 he yielded to pressure and joined the Egypt-sponsored anti-Assyrian confederation which had been formed under the leadership of Ashdod (Azotus). Isaias' denunciation of the alliance[3] was vindicated by events: within a year, Sargon the Assyrian (721–705) had routed the forces of the league and Ashdod had fallen.[4]

But Ezechias had not learned his lesson and, when Sargon died, Juda looked once more towards Egypt and took a prominent place in the ranks of Assyria's declared enemies. Sennacherib, Sargon's successor (705–681), took swift action. Having first settled with Merodach-Baladan, his enemy nearer home, he devoted his attention to the west. Sending a force against Jerusalem to hold it in check, he first broke

[1] Cf. Is. 2. 18–20; 17. 8, etc.
[2] 4 Kg. cc. 18–20; 2 Par. cc. 29–32.
[3] Is. cc. 28–31 probably refer to this alliance.
[4] Cf. Is. 20. 1–6.

the opposition of Juda's allies and then, from his new head-quarters at Lachis, proceeded to the reduction of the cities of Juda while his holding force besieged the capital. Ezechias agreed to pay the indemnity demanded but, assured of divine help by Isaias, refused to surrender the city. Senna-cherib could not afford to wait—events at home had taken an ugly turn and a providential plague had struck his army. He withdrew. Jerusalem was saved (701).

Little is known of the remaining years of Ezechias' reign but after a deliverance so clearly God-sent and foretold by Yahweh's prophet, the prestige of the old religion must for a time have soared. Nevertheless, the national change of heart was to prove shallow and short-lived.

MANASSES, 693–639.[1] AMON, 639–638[2]

The days of Achaz came again: a subdued kingdom paid its Assyrian tribute not only in money but in religious practice. The whole retinue of Assyria's gods again invaded the land of Yahweh and His Temple was desecrated with their immoral worship.[3] Canaanite gods were welcomed too, and the king himself is known to have sacrificed his own son to Moloch. A fierce persecution of Yahwists broke out, in which it is probable that the prophet Isaias perished.

Meanwhile in Niniveh Asarhaddon (681–669) had suc-ceeded Sennacherib, and the Assyrian empire reached the peak of its fortunes when he pushed its frontiers to the shores of the Nile. Under his son Assurbanipal (669–626), however, there was a general uprising in which Egypt re-covered its independence. Babylon, too, rebelled (652) but without success. Manasses of Juda, who had been foolish enough to join in the revolt, was taken prisoner to conquered Babylon. His short term of captivity chastened him and he returned to Juda to initiate a religious reform.

---

[1] 4 Kg. 21. 1–17; 2 Par. 33. 1–20.
[2] 4 Kg. 21. 18–26; 2 Par. 33. 20–25. [3] Cf. Ez. 8. 16 f.; Jer. 8. 2.

Amon, the idolatrous son of Manasses, was not suffered to reign for more than two years; he was assassinated in a palace conspiracy, and Josias, his eight-year-old son, was saluted king in his stead.

Josias, 638–609.[1] Joachaz, 609[2]

The new reign witnessed something of the old Davidic splendour. The rising power of the Medes and Persians on their Iranian plateau was worrying Assyria, and Josias could afford to be more independent than his predecessors. A thorough reform was set on foot which embraced Samaria (626). The Assyrian upstart gods and the old-established Canaanite divinities were alike expelled. But this re-organization, which had been urged by the prophets *Sophonias* and *Jeremias*, was given even greater impetus by an important discovery. In 621, while the builders were at work on the restoration of the Temple, the high priest Helcias found there a copy of "the book of the Law of Yahweh by the hand of Moses".[3] Josias, on reading it, was shocked to find how gravely its solemn injunctions had been violated; it was with redoubled zeal that he set about the restoration of the old religion in all its primitive purity. Well understanding that this purity was best preserved by keeping the Temple at Jerusalem the one legitimate sanctuary, he abolished the abusive sacrifices in the "high places" which had sprung up again throughout the country.[4]

[1] 4 Kg. 22.1—23.30; 2 Par. cc. 34–35.
[2] 4 Kg. 23. 30–34; 2 Par. 36. 1–4.
[3] Possibly the book of Deuteronomy only, but more probably all five books of Moses. Other copies had no doubt been destroyed in the persecution under Manasses.
[4] The principle of the one place of worship (Deut. c. 12) had already been acknowledged when the Ark was the centre of cult, but when the Ark was taken to camp, in time of war, sacrifice was also permitted at its permanent "headquarters" at Silo. From the time of Samuel onwards, the Ark and the Tabernacle were in different places and sacrifice could be offered at either place. Once the Temple was built, it was clear that the condition required by Deut. 12. 9 (social stability) was at last achieved

The people celebrated the Pasch with solemnity and renewed the ancient covenant with Yahweh. The silence of the watchful Jeremias between the years 621 and 608 appears to indicate that things in the religious world were going well.

While the reform was going forward in Juda, the Assyrian empire was on its deathbed. Assurbanipal's prosperous reign was over (626) and in Babylon the Chaldean captain, Nabupolassar (625–605), had secured the throne. Niniveh could not withstand the combined onset of the Medes and Babylonians. The great city fell in 612. The contemporary prophet *Nahum* foretold its fall (Nah. c. 1) and rejoiced in it (Nah. cc. 2–3). The spoils of the fallen empire were divided: Assyria, Armenia, Asia Minor went to Cyaxares the Mede, while Nabupolassar received Mesopotamia, Elam, Syria and Palestine. Egypt had complacently regarded a preoccupied and weakened Assyria, but she took alarm now and marched northwards through Palestine to prop the last refuge of the dying empire in Harran. But Josias saw in Assyria's extinction the hope of his national and religious independence. At Mageddo in 609 he denied passage to the pharaoh. The result was disastrous. The defeat and death of Josias was a tragedy for the cause of Yahweh and provided impressive propaganda for the anti-Yahwist faction whose idolatrous altars Josias had destroyed.

Joachaz, son of Josias, was deposed in favour of his brother Eliakim by the victorious pharaoh who changed the name to Joakim in token of dependence.

---

and that therefore there could be now only one place of sacrifice. It is evident that, at the time of the split of the kingdom, Jerusalem had been considered the one centre of cult (cf. 3 Kg. 12. 26 f.). Ezechias, too, is said to have acted according to the Law of Moses when he abolished the provincial shrines (4 Kg. 18. 3–6). The prophet Amos also had long since condemned the local sanctuaries (Am. 3. 14, etc.). If the contrary practice was tolerated in the northern kingdom (cf. Elias in 3 Kg. 18. 30; 19. 10) it was because of the impossibility of sacrificing in Jerusalem (cf. the royal prohibition in 3 Kg. 12. 28). Josias was therefore no innovator— the law of one centre of worship was already recognized in theory even if it were often violated.

THE MESSIANIC HOPE OF THE PERIOD

I. THE KINGDOM

Isaias, cc. 1–3.—After the bad days of Athalia, the outer forms and ceremonies of Yahweh's worship were resumed in Juda. But Isaias was not deceived. He saw that the inward spirit was lacking (1. 11–18). If the kingdom were to escape destruction, he said, there must be a change of heart (1. 20). In the field of foreign affairs, too, Juda's policy must be revised. There must be one guiding principle: trust in Yahweh (7. 9). Without this, not warlike preparation (2. 8 f.) nor the active pro-Assyrian policy of Achaz (7. 1 f.) nor the suicidal Egyptian alliance of Ezechias (cc. 28–31) would avail to save Juda. But the obstinacy of kings and people was all too clear. Isaias was compelled to announce the doom of Juda. The hour of Yahweh's judgment would come to Juda and leave the kingdom in ruins (3. 25 f.). The scourge was even now descending, and the scourge was Assyria.

Yet Assyria itself would perish (10. 25), for it was not God's purpose to destroy Juda utterly. From disaster a purified "remnant" of the people would emerge (10. 21 f.). God's powerful protection of this chosen few would demonstrate in a new way His ancient royal rights over Israel. As at the Exodus, God "will again choose Israel" (14. 1) and be its King (24. 23). From this faithful remnant He will begin to rebuild the kingdom which will have for its subjects not the idolatrous (30. 22) nor the violent (11. 9) but those who look to Yahweh and follow His ways (30. 20 f.).

Juda alone, then, is to be His kingdom? No, for her brethren in the north will be reconciled (11. 13), and even the people of all the nations will come to find their happiness in the hill-sanctuary of Sion (25. 6). Then the whole earth will be filled with the glory of Yahweh; a new and universal kingdom will rise on the ruins of old enmities (19. 24).

Micheas—This contemporary of Isaias had foreseen the impending ruin of the northern kingdom (1. 6); he saw also the threat to Juda and denounced the vices which, if unchecked, would bring a like disaster to the southern kingdom (cc. 1–3). It appears that his words had some effect,[1] and Juda escaped the fate of Samaria. This escape no doubt accounts for the marked change of tone in the next two chapters[2] of the prophecy (cc. 4–5). The prophet has seen with joy that a reformed Juda has averted destruction and in this he finds some hope for the future[3]—a hope of more profound conversion and of a more lasting liberation. Like Isaias[4] he foresees a universal and peaceful kingdom centred on Sion, its charter the law of Yahweh. Its foundations will be laid by the faithful "remnant" which will survive after great trials (4. 6), even exile (4. 10). The enemies of the kingdom will be finally destroyed (4. 11–13; 5. 6–14).

II. THE KING

Isaias, cc. 1–39.—In the section commonly called "the Book of Emmanuel" (cc. 7–12) Isaias addresses Achaz the king on a matter of policy (c. 7). Achaz, despite his hypocritical protestations (7. 12) is a fawning slave of Assyria's gods. Trust in Yahweh was not practical politics for him. His obstinacy roused the divine anger: the dynasty of David would indeed remain, for God had promised it of old, but its territory would be laid waste. The policy of Achaz would set in motion national disasters of which the Assyrian invasion would be the first (7. 17–25). The kingdom would not see true prosperity until there should come the child

[1] Cf. Jer. 26. 19 and the reform under Ezechias.

[2] The two final chapters of the prophecy (cc. 6, 7) deal with the northern kingdom for the future of which Micheas prays.

[3] It is characteristic of the mind of the Old Testament writers that small triumphs should be regarded as the divine assurance of greater ones to come. Thus, e.g., after a victory in Basan, the psalmist prays (Ps. 67. 29–32) with confidence for universal triumph.

[4] Is. 2. 2 f.

called Emmanuel to whom the kingdom belongs (8. 8), for this child would grow up in a Juda not yet recovered from the misfortunes let loose by Achaz.

"Behold the virgin[1] shall conceive and bear a son and shall call his name Emmanuel. Butter and honey shall he eat,[2] what time he shall know to refuse the evil and to choose the good; for before the child shall know to refuse the evil and to choose the good, the land shall be abandoned. Whereas thou art in fear before two kings[3] Yahweh will bring upon thee . . . days which have not come since the days when Ephraim seceded from Juda.[4]"

Who is this child Emmanuel? The name means "God (is) with us" and, like the names of Isaias' own sons,[5] it is chosen with a purpose. The child is therefore at least a guarantee of God's assistance; the child is the assurance that Assyria will not entirely destroy Juda:

"The waters of the River (Euphrates; i.e. the power of Assyria) . . . shall sweep into Juda in a flood . . . and its spreading margins shall fill the breadth of thy land, O Emmanuel!" (Is. 8. 7 f.).

But the conqueror will not finally succeed:

"Devise a plan and it shall be frustrated . . . because God (is) with us (Emmanuel)." (Is. 8. 10).

From the obscure passage of Isaias we have quoted (Is. 7. 14–17) one thing is clear, that the prophet promises renewed

[1] The Hebrew word (almah) means "a young woman of marriageable age"; the Jewish translators of the second century B.C. (the "Septuagint") rendered it "virgin", "maiden", clearly indicating a virgin-birth of the child.
[2] The figure of speech may indicate that, though pasturage is plentiful enough, the farming of a deserted land is neglected; cf. 7. 21–25. On the other hand (and this serves to illustrate the extreme difficulty of our text) it may indicate the exact opposite, namely, that Eden will return to earth (cf. the "vegetarian" idyll, Gen. 2. 9, and the failure of our first parents truly to "refuse the evil and choose the good", Gen. 2. 17).
[3] Rasin and Phacee, cf. p. 47.
[4] Is. 7. 14–17; trans. Kissane.
[5] The names of Isaias' sons, Shear Yashub (7. 3) and Maher-shalal-hash-baz (8. 3) are translated: A remnant-shall-return (characteristic teaching of Isaias) and Haste-spoil-speed-booty (threat of invasion). The names are portentous (8. 18).

glory for the Davidic dynasty in the coming of a royal heir in whose birth God himself plays an extraordinary part. That the child is of Davidic stock is evident, for the kingdom of Juda belongs to him (Is. 8. 8; and cf. 2 Kg. 7. 14). How aptly he has been called "Emmanuel" is shown by his astonishing qualities: prince of a peaceful kingdom, he will be of surpassing wisdom, father of his people for ever. When, many centuries later, a child of the line of Achaz was born (Mt. 1. 9) of a virgin mother (Mt. 1. 20; Lk. 1. 34, 35), a child at whose wisdom all wondered (Lk. 2. 40, 47), whose coming brought God's peace to earth (Lk. 2. 14), who promised to be with his people for ever (Mt. 28. 20), the early Christians recalled this text of Isaias (Mt. 1. 23): in Jesus it was eminently fulfilled.

Some little time after these prophecies but, as it appears, still in the reign of Achaz,[1] Isaias once more sees the coming chastisement and the survival of the "remnant" (10. 21). In that disaster all the noblest in Juda shall fall like trees before the axe of the woodcutter (10. 34). One living stump shall remain—the stock of Jesse, David's father. From this trunk one sapling shall sprout, a ruler wise and compassionate, uniting all Israel with the gentiles in one peaceful kingdom (11. 1–16).

Micheas—Isaias' contemporary has equal confidence in the dynasty of David. Having warned of the chastisement that must precede the triumph (5. 1) he describes the future happy age in some detail and the figure of the one who is to usher it in:

"Now surround thyself with a wall (Hebr: *gader*), Beth Gader![2] They are setting siege to thee; with a cudgel they are striking the jaw of the tribes of Israel! But thou, Bethlehem of Ephratha, little

---

[1] Cf. the reference to the appeal of Achaz to Assyria in 10. 20.

[2] The prophet is addressing all Juda but selects this one town for the play on its name; there is probably a similar play on the word "Ephratha" (the population of Bethlehem was Ephrathite; cf. 1 Kg. 17. 12) since the Hebrew word suggests "fruitful", i.e. producing (the Davidic prince).

as thou art among the clans of Juda, out of thee there will come
forth for me one who is to be prince in Israel; his origin (is) from
antiquity, from the days of the distant past. He (i.e. Yahweh) will
therefore deliver them over (i.e. Israel, to its enemies) until she
who is to give birth bears the child. And the rest of his brethren
shall return to the children of Israel. He shall stand and shepherd
(them) by the power of Yahweh . . . and they shall dwell (in peace),
for at this time he shall be in great renown even to the ends of the
earth." (Mic. 5. 1–4).

Bethlehem, the birthplace of David, will again produce a
prince. He is himself of David's line, for he can trace his
ancestry back to the early days of the dynasty.[1] The passage
recalls the Emmanuel of Isaias, for Emmanuel too was to
come when Juda was still feeling the effects of enemy invasion. Moreover, the mysterious "she who is to give birth"
reminds us of the "virgin" of Is. 7. 14. The strange promi-
nence given to the mother of the king in these two prophets
is probably to be explained by the importance of the queen-
mother's status in the royal court of Juda (cf. p. 138). As for
the mention of Bethlehem, it is clear that Herod's consultants
had taken the prophet literally (Mt. 2. 5, 6) and the event
showed that they were right.

NOTE: THREE PRE-EXILIC PROPHETS

1. *Sophonias*

Sophonias prophesied nearly a century after Isaias and
Micheas. His prophecy reflects the troubled conditions of his
time ("in the days of Josias", probably about 630 B.C.).
The menace of a great upheaval is in the air (c. 2). The
peril, which threatens Juda also, is not from Assyria, which
is in decline (2. 13 f.) but comes rather from the new
Chaldean dominion in Babylon backed by the expanding
power of the Medes.

"The great day of Yahweh" is near (1. 14) and Juda will

---

[1] Or possibly Micheas refers to the mysterious pre-existence of the
king.

not escape, for its wicked ones will be destroyed (1. 12).
The just will survive (2. 3) to form a faithful remnant (2. 9)
and to constitute God's purified kingdom (3. 12–15). The
kingdom will be independent of political alliances,[1] for its
strength will come from the Lord (3. 12). The nations with
one accord will come to honour the name of Yahweh (3. 9).
A song of triumphant thanks fitly closes the prophecy
(3. 14–20).

2. *Nahum*

Written shortly before 612 B.C., the burden of Nahum's
prophecy is the fall of Niniveh, which marks the end of
Assyrian oppression. This theme engrosses him and he is not
concerned with the distant future; nevertheless, he sees
God's triumphant justice in the fall of Assyria and is confident of the care He takes of Israel, His vineyard (2. 3).
Nahum therefore sounds a note of hope for the future and
his words are taken up in the book of Isaias when the era of
salvation is announced (Is. 52. 7, cf. Na. 2. 1).

3. *Habacuc*

The prophet Habacuc, writing shortly before the Exile
(between 605 and 597 B.C.) is confident of his people's
destiny even when he foresees Juda's chastisement at the
hands of Nabuchodonosor. It is impossible that Yahweh
should allow his people to perish, for it is a people destined
to be the judge of nations:

"Yahweh, thou shalt not cause to perish the one (Israel) whom
thou hast appointed for equity, and whom thou hast established
on a rock for the exercise of justice." (Hab. 1. 12; trans. van
Hoonacker.)

[1] Note the protests of Isaias (30. 16) and of Jeremias (2. 18) in this
regard.

CHAPTER VII
THE KINGDOM IN EXILE AND AFTER

The following biblical books should be consulted:

Historical: 4 Kings, cc. 24, 25; 2 Paralipomenon, c. 36; 1 Esdras 1.1—4.5; 4. 6–23; 2 Esdras (Nehemias), cc. 1–13; 1 Esdras, cc. 7–10.

Prophetical: Isaias, cc. 40–66; Jeremias (with Lamentations); Ezechiel; Aggeus; Zacharias, cc. 1–8; Malachy; Joel; Abdias; Jonas.

Doctrinal: Job; Canticle of Canticles; certain of the Psalms.

I. THE EVENTS
I. BEFORE THE EXILE

The fall of Niniveh in 612 B.C. had broken the power of Assyria for ever, and Nabu-apla-usur of Babylon now held a double sceptre. Of his dynasty, the tenth and the last, his son was the most illustrious member and the most important in Israel's history (Nabu-kudurri-usur, or "Nabuchodonosor", 605–562). As general of his father's armies he had effectively asserted Babylonia's claim to Syria and Palestine by his decisive defeat of the Egyptian army at Carchemish on the upper Euphrates (605).[1] Juda's misguided policy of the next thirty years shows that the new situation was not appreciated: it should have been evident that Egypt would not lightly venture again beyond the frontier.

Joakim (608–597) owed his position as king of Juda to his Egyptian sympathies; the same sympathies were his undoing. Nabuchodonosor, following up the vanquished of Carchemish, secured Jerusalem. Among the hostages sent to Babylon was *Daniel* the prophet (605). Joakim remained to promote open rebellion against Babylon. Egypt made no

---

[1] It was probably at this time that the prophet Habacuc voiced the common fear of the Chaldeans, promising ultimate deliverance.

move. Joakim was dead before Nabuchodonosor could reach Jerusalem, but his son *Joakin* (Jechonias), who reigned for three months, was deported to Babylon with 7,000 of the nobility including the prophet *Ezechiel* (*first deportation*, 597).

Sedecias (597–586), though placed on the throne by Nabuchodonosor, persistently toyed with a projected anti-Babylonian confederation with Tyre at its head and Egypt at its back. The policy was bitterly opposed by *Jeremias* the prophet. This time, Egypt abandoned its isolationism, but its help was ineffective, and Nabuchodonosor, manœuvring to split the Phœnician and Transjordanian allies, moved against Juda. Jerusalem fell in 586 after a siege of eighteen months; an Egyptian attempt at relief had proved ineffectual. Sedecias was led blinded into Babylon—the last king of David's dynasty. The Temple was sacked and burned, the walls and fortifications of Jerusalem demolished. The deportation which followed (*second deportation*, 586) left little more than a population of peasantry in Juda. The prophet Jeremias who had consistently advised a pro-Babylonian policy was allowed to remain, but after the assassination of Godolias, the new governor of Juda, he was forced to accompany the many Jews who, fearing Babylonian reprisals, fled into Egypt. Here, it seems, he was murdered by the compatriots whose impieties he constantly and courageously denounced.

Of the life of those who remained in Juda (perhaps 30,000–40,000 in number) little is known, of their political status, nothing. Jeremias[1] mentions a *third deportation* (582) which must have been provoked by further disturbances, and (in the "Lamentations") describes the distress of those left behind. Their deep-rooted idolatrous tendencies must have been encouraged by infiltrations into the empty land from Moab, Ammon and particularly from Edom.

[1] Jer. 52. 30.

II. The Jews in Exile

The exiles, whose number is estimated at 60,000–80,000, were settled in Babylon itself or in the surrounding district since they were to be used for furthering the works of reconstruction which were proceeding in the capital. Yet in their new home they soon came to enjoy considerable freedom, especially after the death of Nabuchodonosor, and they were not slow to use their opportunities, agricultural and commercial. The Jewish instinct for finance found a happy hunting-ground in the Babylonian money-market.[1] The large donations made later by the Jewish colony in Babylon to the restoration of the Temple and the reluctance of many to avail themselves of permission to return to Palestine are evidence of the Jew's ability to establish himself comfortably in an adopted land.

III. The Return from Exile

The Jews owed their liberation to one of those recurring surprises which make the course of history, humanly speaking, unpredictable. Cyrus the Great (558–529), son of Cambyses of the Achmenid family, was a member of a Persian tribe—the Pasagardæ. The little kingdom of the Achmenids, in the district of Susa, placed itself at the head of a coalition of Persian tribes. By 550 Ecbatana, capital of the Medan overlords, had fallen and Cyrus declared himself "king of Persia". With the collapse of its partner in the sovereignty of Hither Asia, Babylonia at last took fright and its king Nabonid (556–539) made league with the kingdom of Lydia and with Egypt. In 546, Lydia was eliminated when Sardis fell and Cyrus, thanks to the new Persian tactic of archery and cavalry, was master of Asia Minor. In 540, he

---

[1] Excavations at Nippur in the last fifty years have revealed ledgers of the Jewish banking firm of "Murashu and Sons" which carrried on business not only with compatriots but also with Medes, Arameans and Chaldeans in the second half of the fifth century B.C.

turned against Babylonia, whose power had steadily declined since the death of Nabuchodonosor. Its king, Nabonid, had committed the government to his more efficient son Baltassar (Belshassar), but it was too late, and Babylon, the great city whose walls had been a proverb in Asia, succumbed to Cyrus in two days (539).

Cyrus the Persian had none of the ruthlessness of Semitic conquerors. His faith, which was Zoroastrianism, and his political foresight both made him broadminded; indeed, he was more of a liberator than a conqueror, and his tolerant treatment of vanquished states and princes fortified the hope of the oppressed while it undermined the opposition of their oppressors in every place. He came to exiled Juda, therefore, as a deliverer anointed of Yahweh.[1] Within a short time of his occupation of Babylon, Cyrus issued the edict[2] which was to restore the fortunes of Israel.

In 537, the first of the liberated Jews once more crossed the desert, this time in the homeward direction. They numbered nearly 50,000 and included 7,000 slaves—more evidence of the prosperity that had grown in Babylon. In this migration, which was as much religious as national in purpose, it is not unnatural that priests and Levites should be in the majority.[3] Nevertheless, material problems were pressing: a ruined city, a wasted land overrun with hostile bedouin peoples, provision for those whose homes had been destroyed, settlement of claims to the ancestral homes that remained, all these ills clamoured for remedy before the religious restoration could be attempted. The Davidic prince Zorobabel, grandson of Joakin, was leader of the returned exiles. Helped by the ample resources put at his disposal by those who had chosen to remain in Babylon, he devoted the first six months after the return to the urgent material needs.

---

[1] Isaias (45. 1) calls Cyrus "the Anointed—mashiach—of Yahweh".

[2] See the text of the edict in 1 Esd. 1. 2–4 (in Hebrew) and in 1 Esd. 6. 3–5 (in Aramaic).

[3] See the lists in 1 Esd. 2. 1–70; 7. 1–7.

With Josue, the High Priest, who had also returned from Babylon, Zorobabel was now free to address himself to spiritual reconstruction. The altar of holocausts was re-erected, materials were collected for Temple-restoration and, in 536, the foundation of a new Temple was laid on the site of the old. But work had hardly begun when dwindling resources and increasing opposition, not only from the jealous Samaritans, but even from the Jews who had remained behind in Juda, cooled the ardour of the builders and finally caused the work to cease altogether.

The first years of Darius I, king of Persia (522–485), were a period of restlessness in the young empire and an opportunity for independent action on the part of local governors. When, therefore, Zorobabel and his people, reproached and encouraged by the prophets *Aggeus* and *Zacharias*, once more started work on the Temple, no new approach was made to Darius (520). Yet the re-organization of the empire was already under way and new movements within it were becoming suspect. The satrap of Abar-nahara (the new satrapy which included Syria, Phœnicia, Palestine and Cyprus) began to make inquiries, prompted no doubt by the Samaritans. The Jews referred him to the decree of Cyrus which was subsequently discovered in Ecbatana and generously confirmed by Darius. The Temple was completed in four and a half years (in February–March, 515). In outline it was the same as Solomon's which had taken seven years to build, though in view of the resources available and of the speed of construction we are not surprised that it fell far short in splendour. The Holy of Holies was now empty, since the Ark of the Covenant had perished in the general destruction of 586. In the Holy Place stood the gilded wooden altar of incense and one seven-branched candlestick of gold.

But no city was safe without its walls. Under Xerxes I (485–465) the work of building began, but the mixed and hostile population of Samaria again interfered and to their immense satisfaction their counsels prevailed with Artaxerxes I (465–424). The work was prevented by force (446 or 445), and in all probability, the northern wall which defended the city at its most vulnerable approach was completely destroyed; the other walls were rendered useless.

IV. NEHEMIAS AND ESDRAS[1]

With the completion of the Temple in 515, Zorobabel disappears from the stage of Jewish history. The names of his successors in the civil governorship of Juda are not recorded, but the social evils of their regime are known to us from the words of the prophet *Malachy* whose preaching began at this time (450). Reform, social and moral, was a crying need. In 445, the Jew Nehemias, a trusted official at the court of Artaxerxes I, was named governor ("pehah") of Juda with the royal warrant to rebuild the walls of Jerusalem. Despite armed opposition and subtle plots, organized and devised by Tobias of Ammon and Sanballat the Moabite, "pehah" of Samaria, the walls were completely restored within fifty-two days. As in Zorobabel's time, spiritual restoration succeeded material and Esdras, priest and scribe, proclaimed the Law of Moses anew in Jerusalem and called the people to a renewal of the old alliance with Yahweh.

The first mission of Nehemias had lasted twelve years (445–443) but he was to return. Alarming news of moral decline in Jerusalem was brought to him at Susa and he again secured permission to leave for Jerusalem (425). The rumours had not been exaggerated. The reforms so eagerly embraced, among them those relating to the sabbath observance and to marriage, had gravely lapsed. The priesthood itself was infected and many Levites had left their posts to

[1] We have adopted this probable chronological order of the books of First and Second Esdras: 1 Esd. 1.1—4.5; 4.24—6.22; 4. 6–23; 2 Esd. (the whole); 1 Esd. cc. 7–10. This involves the precedence of Nehemias over Esdras and the identification of the Artaxerxes of 1 Esd. 7. 1 with Artaxerxes II, and of the Artaxerxes of 2 Esd. 2. 1 with Artaxerxes I.

live in the country; a son of Jojada, the reigning High Priest,
had married Sanballat's daughter; it was with the permission
of Eliasib, the late High Priest, that Nehemias's old enemy,
Tobias, had set up a branch of his Ammonite banking-
business in the Temple precincts. Nehemias acted with vigour
and success against all the abuses. This is the last we hear of
him.

Esdras, who had worked with Nehemias on the latter's
first mission, does not appear on the second, but in 398 he
set out for Jerusalem by permission of Artaxerxes II (405–
358) at the head of a caravan which numbered probably
8,000–9,000 persons in all. His work, unlike that of Nehemias,
was exclusively and directly religious. For his reforms and for
his insistence on the Mosaic Law Esdras will be remembered
as the founder of post-exilic Judaism.

Despite an appearance of greatness the Persian empire
was rotting. Under Darius III (335–330) the satrapies were
in practice independent and the great army had become a
shadow of itself. The impact of Alexander the Great brought
the empire down in ruins.

II. THE RELIGIOUS ATMOSPHERE
I. THE FOUNDATION OF JUDAISM

"Judaism" is the new condition of Israel as it emerged
from the Exile. Israel is now a religious community rather
than a nation; its constitution has changed and it is no longer
a monarchy; it has a civil governor appointed by the Persian
king and owing immediate allegiance to the satrap of Abar-
nahara. The governor is, in all probability, a Jew, but, as
representative of a foreign power, he is not the centre of
Jewish loyalty. This centre is the High Priest who ad-
ministers the internal affairs of the community on the basis
of the Mosaic Law. How did this religious body crystallize

and survive in the Exile? How did it retain its exclusiveness in the period that followed?

The people of Juda survived as a people. When the northern kingdom suffered exile, the case was different. Exiled Israel was gradually absorbed in the great spaces of Assyria while, through intermarriage and idolatrous contacts with Assyrian colonists, the Israel left at home met almost the same fate. The ten tribes were lost as Juda never was. Certain providential conditions account for the difference. The exiled northern tribes lived in an empire which, for a century, gave no encouraging signs of weakening, but exiled Juda after twenty years saw the beginning of Babylon's decline, and within fifty years the hopeful star of Cyrus the liberator was in the ascendant. Moreover, the door of Juda's home still lay open—Babylon had not colonized Juda as Assyria had colonized Israel—the land was empty of a great settled population. Nor had the reforms of Ezechias and Josias been without permanent fruit in Juda. Yet these reasons could not have been adequate to tell against the despair which must have followed the destruction of Jerusalem and of the Temple, against the growing prosperity in Babylon, against the splendour of Babylonian idolatry, had they not been reinforced by the preaching of the contemporary prophets. Events had confirmed their forebodings of destruction, might they not be worthy of belief when they foretold, as they did, that the ruin would not be complete[1] nor final?[2] Jeremias had announced that after seventy years of desolation would come the end of trial.[3] The voice, too, of the long dead Isaias was remembered, foretelling a happy release through Cyrus and the rebuilding of the Holy City with its Temple.[4]

But it was *Ezechiel*, living and exhorting in the midst of

---

[1] Jer. 24. 1–7; Soph. 3. 12; Ez. 6. 8–9.
[2] Jer. c. 33; Ez. 11. 17–20.
[3] Jer. 25. 11–12.   [4] Is. 44. 28.

the exiles, who preserved a faithful and hopeful remnant in those difficult days. He saw that the adoration of the one image-less Yahweh and fidelity to His Law (particularly of circumcision and sabbath) was the essential condition of Juda's unity and survival ; this forms, therefore, the gist of his teaching. It was useless, he said, to hope that the City would be spared for the sake of the Temple because the Temple itself was defiled with idolatry.[1] The homesick[2] exiles must therefore realize that Yahweh could and would make His sanctuary in the hearts of His people[3] if those hearts acknowledged their guilt and their need of conversion.[4] When the destruction of Jerusalem confirmed his words, the prophet's tone changed to meet the threat of despair—if Juda were to survive, it must be taught to hope. Hence in his subsequent preaching[5] Ezechiel consoles his people with a promise of the destruction of their enemies and with the prospect of Israel's return to its own land. The dead and bleached bones of the nation would rise to a new life.[6]

When the opportunity to return did present itself, cold reason must have hesitated as it weighed the comforts of Babylon against the hazards of the journey and the grim prospects in Juda. Nothing short of high confidence in Yahweh set the nation on its homeward road and its first purpose was the restoration of His Temple and of the ancient liturgy.[7]

The first enthusiasm not unnaturally waned before opposition and difficulty, but when, thanks to *Aggeus* and *Zacharias*, the Temple at last stood again it was Juda's and Juda's alone. Their northern neighbours, the Samaritans, now a mixed population of doubtful orthodoxy, had offered to co-operate and their offer had been refused. Such exclusiveness was no

---

[1] Ez. 8. 5 f.
[2] Read Psalm 136.
[3] Ez. 11. 19; cf. Jn. 4. 24.
[4] Ez. 18. 3 f.
[5] Ez. cc. 25–32; 33–48.
[6] Ez. c. 37.
[7] 1 Esd. 1. 5.

doubt necessary if the purity of Yahwism was to be maintained, but there were other dangers, and the prophet *Malachy* was forced to denounce them. These were the mixed marriages of Jews with idolatrous pagans and the neglect of the Law of which even the priests were guilty. Malachy was the last of the prophets, and Judaism owed its subsequent reforms to Nehemias the governor and to the priest and scribe, Esdras.

The wall which Nehemias built around Jerusalem is a symbol of his work for the racial, and therefore religious, purity of the Jewish people. To this end he strenuously opposed mixed marriages and by consulting the lists of those who had returned with Zorobabel, verified the Israelitic ancestry of the population; some were found to have no claim, and amongst these were three of the priestly families which were therefore excluded from office. Side by side with Nehemias on the latter's first mission worked Esdras, skilled in the traditional Law of Moses which the people had all but forgotten. He belonged to the class of "Scribes" (*sopherim*) which had worked so assiduously on the literary legacy of Israel, the only consolation for the faithful in exile. This Law Esdras caused to be publicly and repeatedly proclaimed in Jerusalem and the nation, with Nehemias at its head, solemnly pledged itself in a new written pact to observe the Mosaic injunctions. By this charter Judaism was finally founded. When Esdras returned as an old man to Jerusalem he found, it is true, the ever-recurrent evil of mixed marriage but was able to prevail upon the people to remedy the disease for themselves. Esdras goes down in Jewish tradition as the father of the scribes and doctors of the Law and is remembered with gratitude as the collector and preserver of the Sacred Books.

The nation of Israel, dedicated to the Law, isolated from foreign influence and localized about Jerusalem, is henceforth people of Juda, or "the Jews".

II. The Messianic Hope

i. *The Kingdom*

The nation was carried safely through the crisis of the Exile not by the promise of mere deliverance, for this prospect was too negative to be effective, but by a conviction, divinely instilled through the prophets, of the greatness of its destiny. This prophetic hope looked, indeed, to the immediate future—to the defeat of present enemies, to the Return from exile, to the re-establishment of Temple worship —but it looked also far beyond these horizons to the distant years when the perfect kingdom of God would be realized in the Chosen People. The process of this establishment would take time, but the happy events of the immediate future would be at once a foretaste and a guarantee of that distant, golden, "Messianic" age; indeed, as they were to be the prelude to it they were in some sense part of it. Bearing this in mind we can understand how Cyrus could be hailed as a "Messiah"[1] and how Zorobabel the Davidic prince could be saluted in Messianic terms.[2]

Jeremias, whose prophetic office opened in 626 B.C. had been, it is true, an unpopular herald of disaster. God's chosen and beloved people had deserted Him (3. 19 f.), Jeremias urged them to repent and to respect that sacred Pact (11. 1–23) which, by its providential discovery in written form[3] claimed their loyalty anew. There was need for national repentance before the calamity should come which threatened from the north (4.5—6.30). His words, it seems, had some effect and the reform under Josias prospered. But once more, under the impious king Joakim, Jeremias was forced to denounce the widespread corruption. This time he threatened chastisement in greater detail: invasion, destruction, exile would punish an obstinate people (7.1—8.12; 8.13—9.21, etc.).

[1] Is. 45. 1.   [2] Zach. 3. 8.
[3] In 621 B.C.; cf. preceding chapter.

When the scourge of God did fall, the prophet consistently advised submission to the conquering power, but without success—indeed he was bitterly persecuted (c. 38). His warnings were terribly confirmed when Jerusalem and its Temple were destroyed. He mourned the calamity in his "Lamentations".

Yet Jeremias was no pessimist. He saw with inspired vision that after seventy years the Exile would have its end (25. 11 f.) and he could therefore write words of comfort to the exiles in Babylon (c. 29). He promised, too, that a new era would begin with Juda and Israel back from their exile and their old quarrel forgotten (3. 14–18; 30. 1–24; 31. 1, 22, 34). In this new age not only the hostile neighbours of Juda (12. 14–17) but men of every nation (3. 17; 16. 19) would be invited to take their place among the chosen people of Yahweh. In this new kingdom of God the spiritual life would be more profound; the Ark itself would be needed no longer (3. 16) for God would make His presence felt in other and better ways. The old Law of Sinai had been engraved in stone, the more perfect Law of the future would be stamped on the hearts of men (31. 33),[1] destined therefore to endure for ever (31. 35–37; 33. 19–26). Man was to have the fullness of God's truth and grace (31. 31–34).

The second part of the book of Isaias (cc. 40–55), called the Book of the Consolation of Israel, has an entirely different background from the first (cf. p. 61). The enemy now is Babylon, not Assyria, the new disaster is the Exile. It is a message of consolation to the exile—"Be comforted, My people!" (40. 1). Deliverance, material and spiritual, is at hand (40. 2–11). Yahweh had, in Abraham, called Israel to be His people (41. 8 f.), the deliverance from Egypt had confirmed this design (43. 16 f.), the new liberation from

---

[1] Jer. 31. 3–34 has been called the most beautiful passage of the whole prophecy and the crown of Jeremias's teaching. No Old Testament passage has been quoted at such length in the New (Heb. 8. 8–12) and it is the source of the term "New Testament" or "New Covenant".

Babylon—Yahweh's work and no other's[1]—would emphasize
His claim to royal recognition (43. 15) in Israel. Beyond
Israel also it would have its effects: the unexpected deliverance and the fact that it had been foretold should convince all
nations that Yahweh alone is God (44.25—45.6).

So much for the material liberation. What of the spiritual?[2]
The third part of the book (cc. 56–66) presupposes in general
that Israel has now returned from Exile. It promises a
spiritual restoration and, because it is spiritual, the people
must be spiritually prepared (59. 1–21) because only the holy
will be fit for the new kingdom (65. 8 f.). The glory of the new
Sion will far surpass that of the old, for the brightness of
God Himself will have dawned upon it. The nations will
reckon it a privilege to walk in that light (60. 1–3) and to
bring presents to the populous and happy city of God (60.
4 f.). The very rapture of the prophet's earlier description—
walls of sapphire, ruby turrets, crystal gates (54. 11 f.)—
clearly suggests a beauty which is not of this earth. It is the
beauty of God's grace and of God's peace (54. 10).

Ezechiel also, in the third part of his prophecies,[3] opens
up this distant prospect of the future which is to come
"after many days" (38. 8). The new regime will be, above all,

---

[1] Note the emphasis laid on this: Is. 41. 4, 13; 43. 3 f; 45. 5 f.

[2] In the mind of the prophet material liberation and spiritual prosperity are interconnected, partly because experience had shown that
spiritual decadence was punished by political subjection, but especially
because Israel could never be considered truly her spiritual self without
the promised land and her Temple, and the spiritual threat of a pagan
occupying power. The prophet sees the two liberations as part of one
single divine plan of which the deliverance from Babylon is but the first
unfolding. The material deliverance is a prelude to the more important
liberation and a consoling hint that it is sure to come; it is more, it is
an actual preparation of the conditions in which full spiritual deliverance
was eventually to be offered. (These conditions the prophet appreciates,
the time of deliverance he does not know.) We need not be surprised,
therefore, when the Baptist who introduces this offer uses the words
already used by Isaias to herald the return from Babylon: "Prepare ye
the way of the Lord, make straight in the wilderness the paths of our
God" (Mt. 3. 3; Is. 40. 3).

[3] Cc. 33–48.

spiritual (36. 24–28) and the spirit of God will be given abundantly (39. 29). In his final vision the prophet sees this new kingdom of God in the form of a magnificent Temple, the house of Yahweh Himself; Yahweh alone is king and a sanctifying stream from the Temple flows over the land, for sanctity is the characteristic of this new order of things.[1]

Aggeus thinks always in terms of the Temple, the building of which was his great preoccupation; it is therefore in this light that he contemplates the distant future. In his second discourse (2. 1–9) he reassures those who are disappointed with the meagre splendour of the new building and impatient for the glorious restoration which they had been led to believe would surpass the glory of Solomon's reign. Aggeus, content with these poor beginnings, sees in them the preparation of a great future—how near, or how far, even the prophets did not know. Of this future he speaks in phrases which suggest a great world-upheaval (2. 6–7) and then this insignificant Temple will be enriched by the gifts of all the nations.[2] It appears that he speaks, like Ezechiel, in symbols of the great moral stature and universality of the Messianic kingdom which is to be a reign of peace under the kingship of Yahweh.

The outlook of *Zacharias* (cc. 1–8) is slightly different; the rebuilding of the Temple had already begun when his first prophecy was uttered (520–518 B.C.), and it is not merely this rebuilding but the whole process of restoration which provides the springboard for his leap into the future. The adoration of Yahweh has been re-established in Jerusalem, it is a step towards the great time when many peoples and great nations will recognize Yahweh as the true and only God (8. 20–23).

The prophet *Malachy* appeared at a time when the

---

[1] Cc. 40–48; cf. also Apoc. cc. 21, 22.

[2] 2. 8, where read: "And the *precious possessions* of all the nations shall come . . ."

Temple-worship was being performed, but by those who, confident in their mechanical fulfilment of legal injunctions, complained that Yahweh was slow to bring the promised blessings (2. 17; 3. 14–15). Malachy has a double answer for them: first, that the sacrifices of which they boast are niggardly offerings of animals maimed and diseased; second, that the intervention of Yahweh, though certain, must await His own good time. The first part of Malachy's prophecy, therefore, promises a new state of things which is to rise above mechanical observance of a Law and which is to bring with it a universal sacrifice to replace the present unclean Mosaic offerings in Israel. It would appear, too, that this sacrifice is to be an unbloody one.[1] The intervention of Yahweh is the theme of the second section (2.17—4.6): God will come to His Temple at last to establish a reign of justice. But the deliverance will not be for Juda only nor for Juda entirely, because even in Juda the wicked will be condemned (3. 3–5).

The date of *Joel's* prophecy is much disputed but it is probably to be placed about the year 400 B.C. The second part of the prophecy (2.28—3.21) certainly refers to Messianic times, to the great "day of Yahweh" when His enemies will be destroyed and His worship established. Yahweh will pour out His spirit in abundance and all will be saved who call upon His name.

ii. *The King*

Jeremias had foreseen the Exile as a punishment of Juda's infidelity. He blamed the impious kings for leading their people astray; nevertheless, God having made His promise to David would abide by it (33. 20–26). The Davidic dynasty would not be destroyed; desolate as the kingdom was, the time would come when a Davidic king would rule, wise and

---

[1] Mal. 1.1—2.16. In Mal. 1. 11 the strictly technical meaning of the Hebrew word is that of bloodless offering of grain or bread.

just (23. 5–8; 33. 14–26). Jeremias described him as a "twig" of David's stock, thus echoing the Isaian idea of the "rod of Jesse" and providing the term that Zacharias was to use (Zach. 3. 8; 6. 12). Just as Isaias had called this king "Emmanuel"—"God-with-us"—so Jeremias called him "Yahweh-our-justice" (23. 6) for his work would be to make the rights of Yahweh recognized and so to procure the salvation of Juda and of Israel.

Ezechiel, like Jeremias, emphasized the recovery of the Davidic dynasty. Speaking to those in exile he declared that the nation had been ruined by its wicked "shepherds" (kings, priests, leaders), but Yahweh Himself would take care of His flock. He would do so through His servant David (that is, one of the Davidic line) who was to be shepherd and prince (34. 23 f.) and king (37. 24). This new David would teach the sheep to walk in peace in the way of God's commandments, and there would be a new and everlasting covenant of Yahweh with His people (37. 26).

Isaias, cc. 40–55—We have seen how deliverance, material and spiritual, is the comforting subject of these chapters written at a time when Israel needed to learn the meaning of suffering. To the double liberation two champions correspond: the one, Cyrus, will restore political independence; the other, the "servant of Yahweh" will break the spiritual bondage not only of Israel but of the whole world. Each is God's instrument, but while Cyrus is a triumphant warlord, the "Servant" is meek and conquers by freely accepted suffering.

The "Servant" appears in four notable passages of the book of Isaias (42. 1–7; 49. 1–9; 50. 4–9; 52.13—53.12). He is the beloved of God, filled with His spirit, preaching the divine law with gentleness but with unflinching firmness (42. 1–7). His mission is to all the earth, a thought which is to be his consolation when his own people fail him; contempt at home will be more than compensated by the homage of kings (49. 1–7).[1] This contempt is more fully described in the third passage: as he faithfully delivers the message of Yahweh, the "Servant" will suffer injustice and violence; there will even be the mockery of a trial (50. 4–9).

The description of the "Servant's" fortunes in the last of these passages (52.13—53.12) is a prelude to the section of the prophecy (54. 1 ff.) which magnificently describes the glory of a Sion restored under the dynasty of David. This description takes the form of a hymn of thanks for Sion's new happiness (54. 1–17) and of an invitation to live worthy of it (55. 1 ff.). All nations will be partners in the new kingdom of God and subjects of David's dynasty. The terms in which the Servant is described suggest that dynasty: his will be the universal homage promised to it (52. 13–15; 53. 12; cf. 55. 3 f.); he is called, too, "a root out of a thirsty ground" (53. 2)—a phrase that reminds us forcibly of the sapling that was to spring up in a desolate country, the offshoot of a Davidic trunk (cf. Is. 10.34—11.1).

Yet the progress of this Servant towards his triumph was to be surprising, even unbelievable (53. 1). His very origin was to be unimpressive (53. 2), his appearance unattractive (53. 2), even repulsive (53. 3 f.); unrecognized for what he truly was, he would die a criminal's death (53. 8 f.). Why? The prophet solves the riddle: had the prize been a material kingdom this would not have been the way to win it; but the prize was higher—men were to be won from sin by the sacrifice of the Servant's life:

> "If he offers his life as sacrifice for sin,
> He shall have prosperity, shall increase his days,
> At his hand the work of Yahweh shall prosper.
> Freed from the agony of his soul he shall see (it),
> (And) his knowledge shall fulfil his desires.
> The just one, my Servant, shall make multitudes just,
> He shall carry their infirmities.

[1] In 49. 7 translate: "to him who is despised, abhorred by the nation". In 49. 3, the word "Israel" is probably a later insertion.

Therefore will I give him multitudes for his spoils,
he shall have hosts for his share of the booty;
Because he handed himself over to death,
Because he was reckoned among the sinners,
Whereas he was bearing the sins of multitudes
And was making intercession for sinners."

(Is. 53. 10–12).

There is no doubt that our Lord took to himself this ideal of fruitful suffering. On the eve of his death he told his disciples: "In me this saying of Scripture is to be fulfilled: He was reckoned among the sinners" (Lk. 22. 37), and he had told them earlier: "The Son of Man has come . . . to give his life as a ransom for a multitude" (Mk. 10. 45). In the first days of the Church the Apostles preached him as the "Servant" (Ac. 3. 13, 26; 4. 27, 30) and the Evangelists recognized Isaias' portrait in him: according to St Matthew, Jesus "took upon himself our infirmities and bore our diseases" (Mt. 8. 17), and for St John he is "the Lamb[1] of God who takes away the sins of the world" (Jn. 1. 29). They had all learned at last the lesson of the "Servant" passages: God's kingdom could not come without suffering; and that it was not to be maintained without suffering ("Take up your cross and follow").

And indeed experience and humble reflection upon it had long been teaching all thoughtful Israelites this very lesson, and would continue to do (cf. pp. 131 and 139). *Psalm* 21, for example, expresses the same thought. It is a complaint, but loving and confident, of one who is in agony. The agony is described in strange detail: surrounded by his enemies the sufferer is reduced to extreme weakness, he is overcome with thirst, he is tied hand and foot,[2] he hears the derision of his enemies and he watches as they cast lots for his garments.

---

[1] It is probable that for "Lamb" we should read "Servant"; the underlying Aramaic word is very similar.

[2] "Tied" according to St Jerome's version from the Hebrew. Vulgate: "pierced".

Nevertheless the Psalm goes on to praise God for the coming of His kingdom to all the nations—a consequence, it would seem, of sufferings endured. The likeness to the "Servant" of Isaias can scarcely be missed. When the Evangelists came to write of our Lord's passion they had already seen something of the fruits of all this accepted pain. It was inevitable that they should see in Jesus the ideal sufferer and speak of him in terms of this remarkable Psalm (Mt. 27. 35, 41, 43). Our Lord himself had put the thought into their minds when he uttered the first words of the Psalm from the Cross (Mt. 27. 46).

In the fourth vision of *Zacharias* (3. 1–10) the suffering of the Exile is over and the prophet looks forward to its aftermath. Josue, the High Priest of Zorobabel's day, appears in filthy garments; clothed with these he symbolizes the distressed little Jewish community back from Exile. The change into festive robes portends the change to be wrought in the community by the advent of one who is here called, as in Isaias and Jeremias (Is. 4. 2; cf. 11. 1; Jer. 23. 5; 33. 15), "twig" or "branch".[1] In a similar vision (the ninth; Zach. 6. 10–15), Josue is crowned; the action is evidently symbolic, as it was in the fourth vision. The crown is the symbol of the royalty of "the Branch", but placed as it is on the head of a priest it implies a union of priesthood and kingship like that attributed to the king in the book of Psalms.[2] This "Branch" is to establish the universal adoration of Yahweh, for he is to "build a temple to Yahweh" and in this building "they that are far off" are to have a part (6. 12–15).

Malachy, in answer to those who are impatient for God's visitation (2. 17) promises (3. 1 f.) that Yahweh will come in person to renew, and doubtless to perfect, the ancient pact with his people. This He does through His messenger (His

---

[1] Zach. 3. 8, where read: "Hear, O Josue, High Priest, thou and thy companions . . . are men who portend that I will bring my servant 'the Branch'". Similarly read "Branch" for "Orient" in Zach. 6. 12.

[2] Ps. 109. 2–4.

"angel") who appears to be identical with Him and yet distinct from Him. This coming is preceded by that of another "angel" whose mission is one of preparatory conversion. This second messenger appears to be identical with the forerunner who is later (4. 5 f.) called "Elias the prophet".

NOTE: THE OTHER BIBLICAL BOOKS OF THE PERIOD

Jonas, *c*. 400 B.C. An inspired book of great doctrinal value, the doctrine being presented dramatically. At a time when Israel threatened to close in on herself and to forget God's love for all peoples, this remarkable and ironical little book pleaded the cause of the Gentiles. God refuses to condemn repentant Niniveh (Assyria, the arch-enemy of Israel) despite the appeal of an Israelite. The kingdom of God is plainly not to be for Israel only.

Abdias, fifth century. This has none of the universalism of *Jonas*; instead it is taken up with God's justice and power as displayed in the misfortunes of Israel's enemy, Edom.

Esther, *c*. 350 B.C. This book, too, is interested only in the fortunes of Israel. It tells how the Jews in the Persian Empire were providentially delivered from persecution (under Xerxes I? 485–465), explaining the origin of the Jewish national feast of "Purim" ("lots", i.e. those which were cast to decide the day of the Jewish massacre; cf. Est. 3. 7; 9. 17–23).

Psalms. A few of the Psalms can be assigned with great probability to the period during and after the Exile. Thus, for example, Psalm 73 laments the destruction of the Temple; Ps. 136 describes the misery of captivity; Ps. 105 prays for deliverance; Ps. 84 celebrates the return; Ps. 106 thanks God for it; Ps. 146 is in thanksgiving for the rebuilding of Jerusalem.

Job, fifth century. The greatest poem of the Hebrew inspired literature. Unlike *Jonas*, written about the same time, it is concerned not with God's attitude to Israel and the nations but with His treatment of individual men. We learn (as Israel was slowly learning) that God's favourites may suffer and that the only answer to suffering here is humble acceptance. This necessary lesson reminds us of God's Suffering Servant in Isaias (p. 81 f.). We begin to realize that God's chosen one when he comes may be—indeed we expect him to be—a man of sorrows.

Proverbs, fifth century in its present form. Like Job and certain doctrinal Psalms this book belongs to the Hebrew "Wisdom" literature which deals with the various aspects of wisdom, human and divine, practical and theoretical. It is a type of literature very different from the urgent preaching and encouraging promise of the prophets, but its exhortation to wise and sober living was designed to prepare Israel for the moral teaching of Gospel times. The kingdom of God is evidently to be composed of the truly wise and its king must be a greater than Solomon, himself the greatest of Israel's sages. The first section of the book (cc. 1–9) poetically represents Wisdom as a person and thus paves the way for the doctrine of Christ as "the Wisdom of God" (1 Cor. 1. 24) and the "Word" (logos) of God (Jn. 1. 1).

CHAPTER VIII

THE KINGDOM AND THE
NEW AGE

I. ALEXANDER THE GREAT AND HIS
SUCCESSORS (332–301 B.C.)

I. ALEXANDER AND PALESTINE

After two substantial victories over the Persians (at the
Granicus, in 334, and at Issus, in 333) Alexander turned
south with a view to the occupation of Phœnicia and the
immobilization of the Persian fleet. With the fall of Tyre
(332) the small Jewish inland community automatically
became part of Alexander's new world.

Of the great changes impending there was still no sign in
that community: its government remained with the High
Priest; its worship still looked to the restored Temple, a
shadow of its Solomonic predecessor; its agricultural life
depended, as before, on land within a twenty-mile radius of
Jerusalem. Alexander's military achievements would scarcely
have found a place in Jewish history had they not opened the
door to a new age—the age of Hellenism.

II. HELLENISM

"Hellenism" is the term for the uniform Greek culture
which spread over Alexander's immense empire. It aimed at
abolishing national cultural boundaries by means of the
elevation or reduction of those cultures to the Greek level.
The most immediate and obvious changes which it brought
about were not in themselves the most important. These
were social, linguistic, architectural. Socially, the Greek city-
state became the model for towns absorbed into Alexander's
empire; each now had its council and each, independent of
its overlord in all but tribute, governed the surrounding

district. Linguistically, a Greek "*koiné*" or "common" dialect came to serve for business and other relations. Architecturally, baths, gymnasia and theatres (all typically Greek institutions) were constructed on the Greek pattern, a model which betrays itself later even in the porticos of Herod's Temple in Jerusalem.

All these things held dangers as well as opportunities for Judaism, but they did not come into direct contact with Jewish religion. This contact was achieved by that aspect of Greek culture which we call Greek religion. In spite of their philosophers the Greek people were polytheists, and polytheism was the natural enemy of Judaism which was rigidly monotheistic.

A not unnatural outcome of polytheism was Ruler-worship. The gods of Greece had acquired their own human, and often immoral, life-story; it could be no great effort to raise the Head of the State to the same level, as was already the fashion in Egypt. The ruler did not object; he welcomed worship if only as a guarantee of loyalty, and so Alexander though privately cynical willingly accepted the deification accorded him by the Egyptians. We shall not be surprised, therefore, if loyalty and worship should come to be confused, that loyalty should come to be thought impossible without worship. In this sense, however, the Jews could never be "loyal". If Judaism remained faithful (as, alone among all the oriental religions, it did) then the clash was inevitable. After a century and a half the clash came.

III. Alexander's Death and Afterwards
(323–301 B.C.)

From Egypt, where he had laid the foundations of the great port of Alexandria, Alexander turned eastwards for the final conquest of the Persian Empire. He died in Babylon, lord of all Asia from the Ægean to the Indus (325 B.C.: cf. 1 Mac. 1. 1–10).

For the next twenty years there was chaos. One of Alexander's generals, Antigonus, stood for a united Empire; others, like Ptolemy son of Lagus, and Seleucus urged division. Ptolemy had seized Egypt and Seleucus had been governor of the Babylonian province. In the subsequent struggle Palestine changed hands many times: it was occupied by Ptolemy in 319, by Antigonus in 315, by Ptolemy again in 313, by Antigonus in 312. At Ipsus in 301 Antigonus fell before a coalition which included Seleucus. Ptolemy, who took no part in the battle, annexed Palestine despite the coalition which had awarded that country to Seleucus. The Seleucid dynasty now reigning in Syria never abandoned its claim to Palestine and repeatedly urged it with armed force. One hundred years later the claim was successfully established.

II. PALESTINE UNDER EGYPTIAN RULE (301–198 B.C.)

The possession of Palestine was vital to Egypt's security: all but invulnerable on the south and west, the northern approaches protected by her fleet, she lay exposed on the eastern flank to a power which might dominate Palestine. A friendly Palestine, too, would reduce Egypt's anxieties and so, apart from the inevitable tribute, Ptolemaic rule was a benevolent supervision; there was no attempt to impose a hellenizing programme.

Nevertheless, the progress of the Hellenistic outlook was unavoidable. Jews home from Alexandria, Greek veterans retired in Palestine, Greek traders on the coast, all were carriers of the new ideas. The first breach in the wall which surrounded Judaism appeared when, under Ptolemy III (246–221), the civil administration of Judea[1] passed from the High Priest Onias II to his nephew Joseph, a member of the

---

[1] The Greek adjectival form becoming common at this time for "the territory of the tribe of Juda".

Tobiad banking family. The Jewish state had therefore lost something of its theocratic constitution and which was worse, the new civil authority fraternized with a power which however friendly was, after all, Hellenistic.

While Hellenism was on its slow and secret offensive in Judea the Jews had gone out boldly to face it elsewhere. The new port of Alexandria was a magnet for the commercial Jew and its pull was strengthened by Ptolemaic encouragement. The colony there came to number 200,000 Jews; its independence was respected by the authorities and national exclusiveness seemed to ensure its religious fidelity, though its active and successful proselytism involved the risk of pagan contamination. That Judaism now was prepared to run that risk is a new and surprising thing. Judaism now displays the ardour not of a new religion but of an old one confident in its excellence and for the first time opening its eyes to its possibilities. Henceforward a Jew will not be thunderstruck if he is told to go forth "and teach all nations".

The great symptom of this new Judaism is the Septuagint —the Greek translation of the Hebrew sacred books made by Jews in Egypt. As in Palestine so in Egypt the Jews had come to forget the tongue in which their sacred books had been written. In Egypt the Jew spoke Greek, and since the Law and the Prophets were read in the synagogue, a Greek translation was imperative, not primarily for the purpose of proselytism but for the benefit of the Jewish community itself. The translation was begun, as the evidence indicates, under Ptolemy II Philadelphus (285–246 B.C.) and completed about 132 B.C. It unlocked to the pagan the treasure of Judaism, hitherto jealously guarded. The true beneficiary of the work was to be the infant Christianity. The Septuagint (or translation of the "Seventy" Jewish doctors, as the story runs) became the Old Testament used by the Christian body; with its help the Apostles demonstrated to the Greek-speaking peoples the Messianic claim of Christ.

III. PALESTINE UNDER SYRIAN RULE
(198–63 B.C.)

I. HELLENISM MOVES TO A CLIMAX (198–166 B.C.)

The dynasty of Seleucus had never conceded Palestine to the Ptolemies. In 218 B.C., Antiochus III ("the Great") had marched through the country but had been decisively defeated at Raphia (217). He returned to the attack in 202 when he succeeded in reducing Gaza, but it was in 198 that he became master of Palestine after having defeated the Egyptians conclusively at Paneion (later called Cæsarea Philippi) near the sources of the Jordan. His magnanimity won him supporters in Jerusalem but others remained faithful to the Ptolemies and opinion in Jerusalem was divided.

The growing power of Rome now began to make itself felt in eastern affairs. At Magnesia in 190 B.C. Antiochus suffered a major military disaster at the hands of Scipio Asiaticus; he was forced to renounce his possessions west of Taurus and to pay an enormous indemnity. Seleucus IV, successor of Antiochus, sought to solve his inherited financial difficulties by an attempt, which proved unsuccessful, to pillage the treasures of the Jerusalem Temple (cf. 2 Mac. 3. 1–40). It was a political blunder which lent strength to the anti-Syrian faction in Jerusalem.

Meanwhile, the peaceful penetration of Hellenism was proceeding. To the north Samaria, already half-populated with non-Jews, had been garrisoned with Macedonians by Alexander the Great. Hebron in the south was occupied by the traditionally hostile Edomites who now called themselves by the Greek name of Idumeans. The whole of the western plain was dotted with Hellenistic cities even to the foothills of the Judean mountains. Only in the north beyond Samaria, in the plain of Esdraelon and on the shores of Gennesareth was there Jewish influence. It is impossible to say how far this surrounding Hellenism would have undermined Judaism itself, since the contest was quickly brought to a climax by open assault.

Antiochus IV Epiphanes (175–164 B.C.; cf. 1 Mac. 1.11— 6.16 and 2 Mac. 4.7—9.29) inherited the huge and heterogeneous Seleucid empire which needed a unifying principle. This principle lay to hand: it was Hellenism which bound all the states in a Greek brotherhood of common language and customs, and united them in the recognition of one protector —the divine monarch. Antiochus was not blind to the advantage, and on his coins he styles himself "Theos Epiphanes" or "God Manifest".

Unfortunately, monotheistic Jewry could present no united front. In Jerusalem there were two factions: one was conservative and pro-Egyptian, it rallied to the High Priest Onias III; the other was hellenizing and pro-Syrian and enjoyed the support of the civil administrators (the Tobiads) whose financial interest now dictated a pro-Syrian policy. The powerful pro-Syrian faction prevailed and Antiochus deposed Onias whose hellenizing brother Jason was named High Priest (173 B.C.).

It is important to notice here the inroads which Hellenism had made into the Jewish constitution. The post-exilic High Priest had held an office which was also civil, hereditary and for life. We have seen the disappearance of the first privilege under the Ptolemies when the Tobiads were entrusted with the civil control; the third has now been ignored by the Seleucids with the deposition of Onias; the second will go within two years (in 171 B.C.) when Menelaus, who was not even of priestly family, would buy the office from Antiochus.

Under Jason's leadership the situation in Jerusalem developed alarmingly. A new Greek gymnasium, set up near the Temple, attracted even the priests to the pagan games; circumcision became a badge of disgrace; Greek manners were everywhere. But there was some revulsion of feeling when Antiochus showed his teeth. Returning from an unsuccessful Egyptian expedition in 168 B.C. he reinstated the unpopular and temporarily ousted High Priest Menelaus and proceeded to pillage the Temple treasures. In the same year he built and garrisoned a Syrian fortress in Jerusalem (probably on the hill to the west of the Temple) called the "Akra". Religious persecution followed. Jewish practice (circumcision, sabbath, sacrifice to Yahweh) was declared illegal; an image of the Olympian Zeus (the "abomination of desolation") was set up on the altar of holocausts and sacrifice was exacted under pain of death (cf. 1 Mac. 1. 57–62; 2 Mac. 6. 2–8). Hellenism had done its worst.

II. THE MACHABEES: JUDAISM ACCEPTS THE CHALLENGE, 168–135 B.C.

The first numerous apostasies were followed by the passive resistance of martyrdom and exile and finally by active opposition (cf. 1 Mac. 1. 63–67; 2 Mac. 6.10—7.42). The movement began in Modin, nearly twenty miles north-west of Jerusalem where the Judean plateau falls westward to the maritime plain. To this isolated village came at last the king's officers. Matathias, an Aaronite by descent, refused to sacrifice, slew the agent of the king and fled with his five sons into the hills. They were soon joined by many exiles from Jerusalem amongst whom was "the congregation of the Assideans" (the Greek form of the Hebrew "Chasidim", or "pious ones"). These are mentioned as a compact body zealous for the Law; they recur in later Jewish history as the "Pharisees", though their relations with the Jewish military leader undergo a considerable change, as we shall see (cf. 1 Mac. 2. 1–70).

i. *Judas Machabee*, 167–161 B.C. (Cf. 1 Mac. 3.1—9.22;
2 Mac. 8.1—15.40.)

Judas surnamed the Hammer (?maqqaba) succeeded his
father Matathias in the conduct of the crusade for Judaism.
An adept in guerilla warfare he repeatedly beat the Syrians
back from the approaches to Jerusalem, twice at Beth-horon
at the north-western approach, once at Emmaus a few miles
to the south of Beth-horon. For the moment Judas was master
in Judea. In December of 165 B.C. he destroyed the idolatrous
altar in the Temple; a new altar was set up and consecrated
and the anniversary of this happy occasion became the
"Feast of Dedication". Menelaus, however, remained High
Priest and the Syrian garrison was not driven from the Akra.

In 164 B.C., Lysias, who had become regent of Syria on
the death of Antiochus IV, once more marched on Jerusalem to the relief of the Akra garrison. He succeeded in
occupying Beth-sur to the south of the city, but was forced
to raise his subsequent siege of Jerusalem by dynastic difficulties in Antioch. He made a truce which conceded religious
liberty and Menelaus, who had been the origin of so much
discontent, was executed (162 B.C.).

The direct assault upon the Jewish religion had, for the
time, failed but the indirect attack continued. An energetic
king, Demetrius I (162–150), now reigned in Syrian Antioch,
and the hellenizing party in Jerusalem presented to him for
nomination their candidate for the High Priesthood, Alkimus.
In 162 B.C. Alkimus was installed with the help of the Syrian
general Bacchides. The Chasidim, tired of the struggle,
accepted the new High Priest who was, after all, of priestly
family. Their hopes were disappointed. Alkimus turned on
them and massacred sixty of their number and the rest fled
to the mountains to rejoin the army of Judas.

The Syrian general Nicanor marching south to support
the cause of Alkimus suffered a resounding defeat and was

himself slain near Beth-horon in February of 161 B.C. It was the last victory of Judas. He fell at Eleasa, defeated by a large avenging force under Bacchides. Two-thirds of his picked force had deserted him and his recent alliance with Rome had been of no avail.

ii. *Jonathan*, 161–143 B.C. (Cf. 1 Mac. 9.28—12.54.)

Though religious freedom had been granted in principle, the crusade was not over. Bacchides had reinstated Alkimus and the hellenizers were once more in power. It was increasingly evident that the purity of the Jewish religion was incompatible with political dependence. With this conviction Jonathan, brother of Judas, took up the struggle. Bacchides soon tired of his guerilla skirmishes with the elusive Jonathan and went home. He returned, but a second discomfiture determined him to negotiate with Jonathan who then turned to the extermination of the "wicked" (the hellenizers) from the district around Jerusalem.

The usual dynastic troubles in Syria gave Jonathan the opportunity of exercising his gift for diplomacy. In 153 B.C. Alexander Balas, reputed son of Antiochus Epiphanes, landed in Palestine; his claim to Syria was sponsored by Rome and actively supported by Egypt. Demetrius I authorized Jonathan to gather an army and to fortify Jerusalem. Jonathan did so willingly. Balas countered with an offer of the High Priesthood. Jonathan, of Aaronic descent, accepted this offer also. He could now confront Hellenism both as head of the nation's armed forces and as its spiritual primate. Demetrius now made a further high—and insincere—bid for Jonathan's support. Jonathan refused it, and wisely, for the cause of Balas prevailed (150 B.C.).

By 145 B.C. Balas was dead and Demetrius II (145–138) ruled in Syria. Demetrius had broken faith with Jonathan who thereupon used his forces to support the Syrian general Tryphon who was marching on Antioch with the ostensible purpose of seating the young son of Balas on the throne. Tryphon proved useful. He conferred on Simon, Jonathan's brother, the military supervision of the Palestinian coast from Tyre to the Egyptian frontier. Simon used the golden opportunity to reduce Askalon and Gaza and later (this time, outside his mandate) the now Syrian fortress of Beth-sur which threatened Jerusalem from the south. Tryphon, who coveted the Syrian throne and feared the extending power of Judea, treacherously made away with Jonathan. Rome, with whom Jonathan had recently renewed the alliance, did nothing.[1]

iii. *Simon*, 143–135 B.C. (Cf. 1 Mac. 13.1—16.24.)

The brother of Jonathan immediately assumed control in Jerusalem. He offered alliance to Demetrius II, who still controlled the northern provinces of Syria, in return for remission of tribute. This concession, which meant complete political independence for Judea, was followed by the long-desired capitulation of the Akra. Simon improved the occasion by establishing Jewish dominion over Gazara and Joppa, so providing Judea with an outlet to the sea.

In Simon and his family the priests and people of Jerusalem solemnly invested the High Priesthood, coupled with the rank of Prince "until a trustworthy prophet should arise" (141 B.C.). From this cautionary phrase it appears that the arrangement was not intended to be permanent, nor was Simon styled "King"—the kingship had been long promised only to the Davidic line and evidently the Davidic Messianic hope was not dead.

[1] The Qumran community (cf. p. 123) maintained that a priesthood conferred by a pagan on one who had deserted the crusading ideals of Macchabean days had fallen into the wrong hands. It is probable that the "Wicked Priest" mentioned in the Scrolls was Jonathan himself and that he attempted to suppress the community of Qumran with its head the "Teacher of Righteousness" but was duly punished for this by his violent death in 143 B.C.

Simon was now strong enough to refuse the demands upon Judea's independence made by Antiochus VII (138–129). Two years later (in 135 B.C.) Simon was treacherously murdered by his son-in-law at the fortress of Doq, near Jericho.

With the last of the Machabees we bid farewell to the old crusading spirit and meet the new dynastic ambition which leads to territorial expansion abroad and to division at home. The new dynasty gradually moves away from the conservative Judaism which the Machabees had set out to vindicate.

III. THE HASMONEANS: POLITICAL EXPANSION; INTERNAL DIVISION (135–63 B.C.)

i. *John Hyrcanus* (135–104 B.C.)

Son of Simon and first of the "Hasmonean" dynasty, so named after Hasmon of Juda, the ancestral home of Matathias, John inherited the civil control and the High Priesthood.

The first years of his reign were militarily unfortunate. Antiochus VII, securing his rear for the Parthian war, had occupied Jerusalem (134 B.C.), imposed an indemnity and constrained John to support him against the Parthians. In 129, however, Antiochus was killed, and from that date until 63 B.C. domestic troubles kept Syria out of Palestine.

On his return from the Parthian campaign Hyrcanus besieged and captured Madaba in Transjordania. He then proceeded to pierce the barrier between the reawakened Judaism of the south and the remnant of Israel in Galilee— the territory of the Samaritans. Marching through the vale of Sichem he captured the town of that name and, in 129 B.C., destroyed the schismatic temple on Garizim which had stood since the days of Nehemias. Twenty years later (in 107 B.C.) Samaria itself, political capital of the Samaritan province, succumbed to a siege of one year's duration. The fall of Scythopolis which took place at the time of the siege of Samaria provided Hyrcanus with a dominating position on the plain of Esdraelon and with an approach to Galilee.

Meanwhile, the dominion of Judea had been extended in the south where circumcision had been forced on the defeated Idumeans. Territorially the Jewish kingdom was reaching the peak of its fortunes.

The domestic policy of Hyrcanus was not so happy. His earlier relations with the devout conservative party had been of the friendliest, but the bitterest opposition supervened. The fact is certain, the details are not, but the cause of the split may be conjectured with some probability. The devout party, named in Machabean times the "Chasidim" and now appearing as the "Pharisees" (or "Separatists"), stood for the Law and for the traditions which had accrued to it; their orthodoxy attracted the support of the people. Their natural opponents were the "Sadducees" (a title which also appears at this time). These were the priestly aristocrats who, through membership of the High Priest's council, had come into regular contact with the Hellenistic power and had contracted liberal tendencies. The Pharisees were no doubt jealous of the Sadducees; they felt that the share of their party in the Machabean revolt had earned them the place amongst the king's advisers which was actually filled by the undeserving Sadducees. No doubt, too, they resented the authority of Hyrcanus in spiritual matters which they felt to be their own sphere. Moreover, Hyrcanus had offended their Legal conscience by his employment of foreign mercenaries in the Jewish army. During this and the next two reigns these descendants of the supporters of the Machabees were at loggerheads with the Hasmoneans.

ii. *Aristobulus I* (104–103 B.C.)

Prince and High Priest, son of Hyrcanus, his Hellenistic sympathies served to widen the breach with the Pharisees, nevertheless he forced circumcision on the conquered Itureans (probably in Upper Galilee).

iii. *Alexander Jannæus, King* (103–76 B.C.)

Brother of Aristobulus, he was the first of the dynasty to take the title of King—evidently the Davidic scruples of Simon's day were not powerful enough to hinder the assumption of the royal title. The Pharisees, in any case, would have no say in the matter.

Alexander's reign is remarkable for wars at home and abroad. At home he was a most unpopular High Priest, and when the hatred of the Pharisees reached its climax there followed a six years' civil war. While Alexander enrolled foreign mercenaries against his own people, the Pharisees called in Demetrius III of Syria. Alexander, on the brink of defeat, was saved by the desertion of many of the rebellious Jews to his cause. He exacted a terrible revenge: eight hundred of the Pharisees were crucified and ten times that number fled into exile. For the last twelve years of his reign Alexander had peace at home.

Abroad the Jewish State expanded. Galilee in the north, on the west the maritime plain from Carmel to Egypt, east of Jordan the hellenized towns of Gadara and Pella and Gerasa, all were occupied and confronted with the alternative of circumcision or extermination. As in the case of Aristobulus this policy was rather national than religious—a disquieting perversion of circumcision's original purpose.

When Alexander died (in 76 B.C.) his territory embraced Idumea in the south, a considerable part of Transjordania stretching to the north of Gennesareth, Galilee and the Mediterranean coast from Mount Carmel to the Egyptian frontier (with the exception of Askalon).

iv. *Alexandra* (76–67 B.C.)

Alexander's widow reversed her husband's domestic policy. She restored to the Pharisees the authority in legal

matters which had been annulled by Hyrcanus. Pharisaism
points to her reign as its golden age, and from now, on
through the time of our Lord and beyond, Pharisaism is the
authorized spokesman of official Judaism.

During Alexandra's reign her elder son, Hyrcanus II,
filled the office of High Priest; the younger, Aristobulus
directed military affairs. With the strong support of the
Sadducees Aristobulus was in a position to snatch the
kingdom and the High Priesthood from Hyrcanus four
months after their mother's death.

v. *Aristobulus II* (67–63 B.C.)

Hyrcanus would have been content to live in retirement
but Antipater, a prominent and ambitious Idumean, father
of Herod the Great, persuaded him to an offensive alliance
with the Transjordanian Arabs. Joined by the Pharisees they
marched against Aristobulus and his Sadducee supporters
in Jerusalem. But the Roman Pompey was already in Asia,
and in 65 B.C. he sent his lieutenant Scaurus to investigate
the Judean disturbances. The Arabs were peremptorily
ordered to raise the siege and Aristobulus was summoned
to appear with Hyrcanus before Pompey in Damascus.
Aristobulus and Hyrcanus were joined by a third delegation
which came to represent the feeling of the people (and of the
Pharisees) who wanted no king at all but only a High Priest.

Though Aristobulus had surrendered himself to Pompey,
his supporters still held out in Jerusalem. The city fell to a
three months' siege in 63 B.C. Pompey, having confirmed
Hyrcanus in the High Priesthood, took Aristobulus back to
Rome with him to grace his triumph.

The new Jewish State was reduced to Judea, Galilee, a
small part of Transjordania (Peræa) and a few districts of
Idumea. The cities of the coast were annexed to the new
Roman province of Syria. Hyrcanus became "ethnarch" of

the limited territory; he was responsible to Scaurus in Syria.

Henceforward Judea was governed either by a Roman "procurator" or by a prince answerable to Rome.

IV. BIBLICAL MESSIANISM OF THE HELLENISTIC PERIOD

I. THE KINGDOM

To the period immediately following the death of Alexander the Great in 323 B.C. belongs, as it seems, the second half of the book of *Zacharias* (cc. 9–14). This looks forward to the time when idolatry will be no more and (reminding us of the prophecy of Ezechiel, p. 79) there will be a sanctifying fountain for the cleansing of sin. Yahweh alone will be king of the whole earth. The prophecy ends (c. 14) with a tableau so extraordinary that it betrays its symbolic character: the mountains of Juda are levelled and a new Jerusalem dominates the plain. Holiness pervades the whole kingdom, for even on the bridles of the horses are written the words once reserved to the headdress of the High Priest: "Holy to the Lord" (14. 20; cf. Ex. 39. 29 f.).

The book of *Daniel*, which we may date between 167 and 164 B.C., belongs in part to the type of literature known as "apocalyptic", a style of writing immensely popular in the last two centuries before Christ. The "apocalypse" (i.e. "unveiling") set itself to reveal the working out of the divine plan in the past, present and future. Its purpose was to encourage such as might doubt that God had a guiding hand on history or that He would personally intervene in the future. The purpose of the Daniel apocalypse is to show the divine plan that runs through history and so to console the nation, persecuted by Antiochus Epiphanes, with the promise that the last empire, rising on the ruins of those that have passed, is to be the Kingdom of God. It makes free use of symbols, and the four successive oppressors of Israel, Babylon, Media,

Persia, Greece, appear as four savage beasts. Their power will not last, for they will be succeeded by an everlasting and universal kingdom which is to have saints for its subjects (7. 22). The symbol of this last kingdom is not a beast but "one like a son of man" (7. 13). For Daniel the subjects of the kingdom are primarily the saintly ones among the Jews, but he insists on dispositions that are incompatible with national pride and exclusiveness. The kingdom, therefore, is open to all holy ones. This conception was later to remain unappreciated by the Pharisees.

The same inspired writer goes on to speak in mysterious terms, which allude to the persecution of Antiochus and yet look to a future beyond it (9. 24–27), of "seventy weeks" that are to elapse before "vision and prophecy are fulfilled" and "a holy of holies anointed". The oracle proceeds:

> "From the moment the word went forth: 'Return and rebuild Jerusalem', to the coming of an anointed prince, seven weeks; and during sixty-two weeks, squares and ramparts rebuilt but in a time of trouble. And after the sixty-two weeks, an anointed one cut off (and?) city and sanctuary destroyed by a prince who will come. Its (his?) end shall come in a flood and to the end there shall be war and the decreed catastrophe. And he shall make strong alliance with many for one week; and for half-a-week he shall make sacrifice and offering cease, and on the wing of the Temple there shall be the abomination of desolation until the end, the end decreed for the destroyer."

This enigmatic text whose very translation is difficult and unsure may be explained in the following fashion.[1] Forty-nine years had elapsed between the destruction of Jerusalem in 586 B.C. and the liberating edict of Cyrus (the "Anointed" —"Christos"—of Is. 45. 1) in 537. A period of "sixty-two weeks" (actually about 370 years) then followed, during

[1] Remembering (1) that the "weeks" are of years, i.e. each "week" is equivalent to seven years. (2) that the number 70 is a round number used by Jeremias (25. 11) for the period of Exile and adopted by Daniel. (3) that this number here describes three periods, the first and last of which are historically precise, leaving the middle period necessarily approximate—in reality nearer 52 than 62 "weeks".

which time Jerusalem was reconstructed. The Syrian persecution followed in 168 B.C. when sacrifice in the Temple was suppressed for "half-a-week" (3½ years; 168–165). The murder of the "Anointed" High Priest (Onias III) actually took place in 171.

It is evident, despite all obscurities, that for Daniel the events of those years are a prelude to the coming of the kingdom; the inspired writer is confident that iniquity will be shortly abolished and vision and prophecy fulfilled (9. 24). We notice once more that suffering and distress are associated with the Kingdom's coming. And in effect the Syrian spoliation of the Temple ("the abomination of desolation") was repeated by the Romans in 70 A.D. (cf. Mt. 24. 15) when another Anointed had been slain. But after this Roman destruction of the Temple the Christians knew that they had with them the risen Jesus, a new and indestructible Temple (Jn. 2. 21), an anointed "holy of holies".

II. THE KING

In the second half of the book of *Zacharias* (cc. 9–14) the future king's reign is represented as a peaceful one; weapons of war are henceforth useless and so destroyed. The king enters his capital, Jerusalem, on an unwarlike beast to rule a world-wide empire (9. 9 f.). Then in a mysterious passage full of the promise of a coming age of grace an obscure figure appears:

"On David's house and the dweller in Jerusalem
I will pour out a spirit of loving kindness and prayerfulness.
They shall look upon him who has been pierced;
they shall make lamentation over him
as men weep for a first-born child.
In that day there shall rise great lamentation in Juda . . .
In that day there shall be a fountain opened for David's house
and for the dwellers in Jerusalem, for sin and for uncleanness."

(Zach. 12. 10; 13. 1.)

The effusion of grace is the result of the suffering and death of one who is "pierced". Once more, as we have seen so often, a connection is established between suffering and the coming of God's Kingdom of grace. St John, witness of our Lord's death, witnessed also the piercing of his side with a spear and the effusion of blood and water, symbolizing the Holy Eucharist and Baptism. Remembering this, he recalls the words of Zacharias: "They shall look upon him who has been pierced" (Jn. 19. 37).

That *Daniel* pictured the great empires as savage beasts, we have already seen. In sharp contrast, the coming empire of God is portrayed as "one like a son of man". Daniel himself (7. 18, 22) identifies this "Son of Man" with "the saints of the Most High", the subjects of God's future Kingdom. Nevertheless, in ancient times a kingdom was unthinkable without its king and the symbol of one was the symbol of the other, as indeed the beasts are in Daniel (7. 17, corrected reading: "These four beasts are four kings"). Moreover, the ancient Hebrew prophetic tradition did not visualize the foundation of the kingdom without the anointed king who was to found it. In this sense, too, the Jewish Book of Henoch (cf. p. 106) understood our passage. This "Son of Man" in Daniel's vision (7. 1–18) is seen in heaven riding on the clouds to the "Ancient of Days" from whom he receives a kingdom universal and indestructible. The "coming on the clouds" is not here to be taken literally as if the kingdom were to be established by the sudden appearance of this figure in the air; it symbolizes rather the heavenly origin of king and kingdom. It is to be noted also that this vision, like the others, is presented in the form of a tableau which takes no account of the time element; it is therefore quite compatible with the *gradual* establishment of the kingdom. It is in this sense that the Sanhedrin would understand the words of Jesus in Mk. 14. 62.

The phrase "Son of Man" became our Lord's favourite

title for himself; it had the advantage of calling attention to the simple human state he shared with all mankind and, at the same time, of suggesting a heavenly origin, more than human, and a royal title divinely conferred. For the first, cf. Mt. 8. 20; 11. 19; 20. 28 f. For the second, cf. Mt. 17. 9; 24. 30; 25. 31, but especially Mt. 26. 64 where he solemnly invokes our passage of Daniel to show that his Messiahship is by no means political but heavenly in origin and in purpose.

V. NON-BIBLICAL MESSIANISM OF THE HELLENISTIC PERIOD

Of the uninspired apocalypses it may be said in general that their pictures of the future happy age are material and grotesque. Though their canvas is the whole universe, it does not appear that their nationalism is any the less exclusive. It is true that they treat of the destiny of all humanity, but in doing so they either condemn the Gentiles altogether or grudgingly grant them a place in the future happiness only on condition that they become servants of Israel. In this, as in their whole notion of God's relations with man, they fall far short of the width and depth found in the doctrine of the Prophets.

Nevertheless, the books are a valuable link between the Old Testament and the New; they at least serve to show how intense was the Messianic hope in the two centuries before Christ. This intensity, it may be noted, was due particularly to two causes. The first was the political oppression and the persecutions of the second century; these inflamed the desire and nourished the hope of deliverance. The second was the surprising victories of the Machabees; these seemed to make the hope realizable.

But it is evident from the apocalypses that the Messianic idea, though ever present, was conceived differently in different circles and at different times. Thus the future Kingdom which they describe is now temporal, now eternal;

at one time a personal Messias appears, at another he falls
completely into the background.

Thus, for instance, parts of the Book of Henoch (? 150 B.C.)
present a tableau of victorious wars which appear to be the
Machabean wars. This is followed by a purification of the
earth preparatory to the final judgment. Of a personal
Messias who will produce these things there is no mention
whatever. Yet in another part of the same book (?160 B.C.)
an individual Messias is clearly symbolized by the figure of
a white bull with great horns. This figure appears after God
has personally overthrown and punished the sinners of the
world and has come to dwell with His people in Jerusalem.
The function of the Messias is merely to rule over this new
world of peace which the action of God has brought into
being. Of the origin of the Messias nothing is directly said,
but it is evidently earthly. Nothing at all is said of his
Davidic connexions, it therefore looks as if the clear prophecies of a Davidic Messias were being conveniently over-
looked at a time when the more immediate hopes of the
nation were centred on the Levitical family of the Machabees.
In this part of the book, as in the first, there is no question
of "the world to come"—all takes place on earth. Yet it is a
new, or rather renewed, world of innocence; it is a return to
the conditions of the days before the Fall. The Messias who
presides over it is a new Adam, for he is represented by the
same symbol—Adam, too, figures as a white bull.

The rather later book of Jubilees (? 125 B.C.) seems to
belong to the early days of the Hasmonean successes. It
confidently looks forward to a national Jewish kingdom on
earth but sketches no picture of an individual Messias. Here
also the traditional Messias of the tribe of Juda is over-
looked; we even observe a preference for the tribe of Levi
from which the Hasmoneans were sprung. The author seems
content with the present state of affairs which promises to
develop favourably for Israel. This outlook warns us how

the distortion of one aspect of the Messianic hope leads naturally to a distortion of another: emphasis on the political nature of the new Kingdom has led to a suppression of the clearest characteristic of Messianic prophecy—the Davidic origin of the Messias.

The tendency is not corrected in the Testament of the Twelve Patriarchs (? 125 B.C.). Here again there is a very small place, if any, given to an individual Messias, but there is an even greater insistence on the glory of the ruling Levitical dynasty of the Hasmoneans. Once more we begin to suspect that the prophetic Messias of Juda is being forgotten.

To conclude: there was evidently at this time a strong conviction of approaching deliverance and of Israel's triumph. This deliverance is sometimes considered as already begun by the successes of the Machabees and of their descendants. Of the personal Davidic deliverer promised by the prophets there is, however, no certain trace, and we have to await the Psalms of Solomon (about 50 B.C.) for a clear picture of the coming Davidic king.

NOTE 1

THE INSPIRED "WISDOM BOOKS" OF THE PERIOD

i. *Ecclesiastes*

Written in a late form of Hebrew, probably at Jerusalem between 300 and 200 B.C. It teaches the vanity of earthly goods and the value of true wisdom. The alleged influence of Greek philosophy has been much exaggerated. The author is not a sceptic, for he praises wisdom (2. 13), nor is he an Epicurean for he condemns the search for pleasure only if it be absorbing and divorced from the fear of God (2. 1; 7. 14 f.). Job had wrestled with the problem of pain, Ecclesiastes investigates the problem of pleasure. It notes that this is deceptive and passing, and by showing the insufficiency of earthly joys it prepared the Jewish mind for the fuller revelation of the future life. It is only a step from "Blessed are not the rich" to "Blessed are the poor" (Lk. 6. 20).

ii. *Ecclesiasticus*

Written at Jerusalem, *c.* 200–180 B.C. The author was Ben Sirach and the work was translated from Hebrew into Greek by his grandson shortly after 132 B.C. It is a practical moral guide and praises particularly the divine wisdom manifested in the Law. The author, though certainly familiar with contemporary Greek philosophy, is not substantially influenced but remains an exclusivist Jew, hostile to surrounding paganism (Ecclus. 36. 1–9; 50. 25 f.). The book has nothing to say about the future kingdom but it pleads with God to remember His promises and to gather together once more the tribes of Jacob. This dream of "ingathering" had haunted the prophets, but Israel refused the offer when it came (Mt. 23. 37).

iii. *Wisdom*

Written in Egypt, probably at Alexandria, 150–50 B.C. It praises divine wisdom as manifested in the history of Israel, contrasting it with the foolishness of idolatry; for proof of this it compares Egypt's unhappy fate with Israel's good fortune. In the clarity of its doctrine of Immortality it far excels the other books of the Old Testament (cf. cc. 3–5). Its language is Greek, like certain of its ideas[1]—for example. it depicts divine Wisdom as a spirit penetrating and yet containing all things—but its doctrine is strictly Jewish, scornful of Egyptian idolatry (c. 15.). Its purpose was to console the Jews in Egypt and to confirm them in their faith. It may also have had the secondary motive of proselytism. The

---

[1] Inspiration guarantees against error, but it does not forbid the human author to use pagan terms or ideas which, in their application, contain no error.

book's long description of Wisdom (7. 22–8. 8), "a spotless mirror of God's work, an image of His excellence", prepares us for our Lord "the wisdom of God" (1 Cor. 1. 30, and cf. Col. 1. 15–16) and God's incarnate Word (Jn. 1. 1 ff.).

NOTE 2

THE INSPIRED HISTORICAL BOOKS OF THE PERIOD

i. *First Book of Machabees*

An Aramaic or Hebrew work composed in Palestine about 100–63 B.C. It is an ordered history of the years 175–135 B.C. written by a Jew profoundly conscious of the sanctity of the Temple and of the Law.

ii. *Second Book of Machabees*

A Greek work composed probably in Egypt not long after 124 B.C. It is a history covering the years 180–161 B.C. Its Jewish author wishes to convince the Alexandrian Jews of their close bonds with Palestine by describing the heroic resistance to persecution on the part of the Palestinian Jews.

CHAPTER IX
THE KINGDOM AND ROME

The intervention of Pompey marked the end of eighty years of Jewish political independence. The legate of Augustus in the new Roman province of Syria now stood ready with his legions in Antioch to guarantee the continuance of this new order. The inevitable tribute was imposed and the Jewish State lost the whole of the coastal region from Carmel to the border of Egypt together with Samaria and the Hellenistic cities of Transjordania.

I. RISE TO POWER OF ANTIPATER THE IDUMEAN
63–44 B.C.

Revolt was not long delayed. In 57 B.C. Alexander, son of Aristobulus II, was defeated in his first attempt and for the next ten years Judean territory was administered from Syria, all administrative power having been withdrawn from Hyrcanus. But private Hasmonean disputes were giving way to national uprising and Alexander was able to muster an army of 30,000 Jews which was, however, defeated heavily near Tabor. Rome was proving a more formidable enemy than Syria had been in Machabean times.

Meanwhile Antipater, the power behind Hyrcanus, was thriving on Jewish discord; it threw into relief his own loyalty to the Roman authority in Syria to whom he had contrived to make himself useful on more than one occasion.

By 49 B.C. Julius Cæsar was master in Rome, but Pompey, in Antioch, was still to be reckoned with. It was a problem for Antipater the diplomat. He waited. Pompey, fearing danger from the south, had Alexander the Hasmonean executed in Antioch while his supporters in Rome poisoned the captive Aristobulus II whom Cæsar had planned to send with two legions into Palestine. Antipater, and with him, of course, Hyrcanus, was thus thrown for a time into the arms of Pompey, but Cæsar's victory at Pharsalia (47 B.C.) found the Idumean prompt to court the victor's favour by giving Cæsar valuable help in his subsequent difficulties in Egypt. From that date Rome, and particularly Cæsar, had a great regard for the family of Antipater.

Reward followed swiftly. Hyrcanus became "ethnarch" (ruler of the nation) in 47 B.C.; Antipater, always virtual ruler, now received the official title of "procurator". Cæsar's further concessions included permission to rebuild the walls of Jerusalem thrown down by Pompey, the restoration to the Jewish State of the port of Joppe, and a military command for the sons of Antipater—Herod in Galilee and Phasael in Jerusalem.

It is not surprising that the Jews loudly lamented the death of Cæsar (44 B.C.); he had set Herod on the high road to power but they could not foresee what this was to mean for them.

II. Herod's Early Career

Herod had energy and diplomatic ability, and there was opportunity for both. As in Jonathan's day, the ruling power was beset with domestic difficulties, but Herod was not in Jonathan's happy position to barter support for concessions, and his Roman policy was perforce more passive though equally astute. He hastened to pay tribute to the greedy Cassius, now supreme in the East, and in return was named governor of Coele–Syria. In 43 B.C. his father Antipater was dead—poisoned by an adventurer—and trouble broke out again in Palestine. Herod defeated the Hasmonean Antigonus and entered Jerusalem.

The defeat of Cassius at Philippi (42 B.C.) presented Herod with another problem, but he succeeded in winning the favour of the victor, Antony, who appointed him and his brother tetrarchs (governors) of the province of Judea. Hyrcanus remained High Priest.

In 40 B.C. the Parthians took advantage of Antony's absence in Egypt to invade Syria; they were joined by Antigonus who occupied Jerusalem. Phasael and Hyrcanus were made prisoner; the former committed suicide, the latter had his ears cut off to render him unfit for the High Priesthood. Antigonus was declared King and High Priest.

Meanwhile the wily Herod had escaped. In the late autumn of 40 B.C. he was already in Rome reminding Octavian of the old friendship between his father Antipater and the adopted father of Octavian, the great Julius. Before the year was out, the decree naming Herod King of Judea was in the Capitol and Herod set out immediately to give effect to the decree by force of arms. But the nationalism of Judea rallied aristocracy, priesthood and people to the side of the Hasmonean against the Rome-sponsored foreigner from Idumea. The campaign dragged out for three years (40–37) and it needed Roman reinforcements from Syria to turn the scale. Jerusalem fell after a five months' siege and Antigonus was taken to Antioch for execution. Herod was King of the Jews.

III. Herod the Great, 37–4 B.C.

The policy of the new king was conditioned by the fluctuation of Roman affairs, and by the constant danger, real or imaginary, of conspiracy at home. After 31 B.C. the first difficulty left him, the second was with him to the end.

i. *Relations with Rome*

Before the battle of Actium in 31 B.C. Herod's situation was delicate. He was in no geographical position to refuse Antony his support: to the north was Asia and Antony, to the south lay Egypt, country of Antony's consort Cleopatra. It was Cleopatra who, with an eye to a kingdom in Palestine, unwittingly extricated Herod from his difficulty. She persuaded Antony that he had no need of Herod's support, for she feared that the gratitude of a victorious Antony might then have confirmed Herod in his kingdom to her disadvantage. However, it was Augustus who proved the victor, and Herod who, thanks to Cleopatra, had not compromised himself at Actium, was quick to conciliate his favour. His reward was a kingdom as great as David's. Augustus bestowed on him the districts given by Antony to Cleopatra which included Jericho, Gaza and Samaria. Later (in 23 B.C.) Herod received the districts of Batanea, Trachonitis and Auranitis.

Herod returned the friendship of Augustus to adulation point. He dotted the country with temples to Rome and Augustus where sacrifice was offered to the statue of the Emperor, notably in Samaria, Cæsarea Palestinæ and Paneion (Cæsarea Philippi).

ii. *Herod and his People*

At home, Herod was the oriental despot. The Jewish aristocracy, natural allies as they were of the Hasmoneans, were the first to suffer. Their massacre weakened the Sanhedrin which henceforth lost the legislative power which it had enjoyed under Hyrcanus I. The new advisory council was made up of Herod's relations and friends. The priesthood was alienated by his capricious deposition and appointment of High Priests. The Pharisees, reflecting and dictating the popular feeling, were shocked by the Hellenism which could erect pagan temples and, in Jerusalem, a new amphitheatre which recalled the bad old days of Antiochus Epiphanes. Herod succeeded in monopolizing the Jewish antagonism which might have been reserved for Rome.

The expensive taste for building which, to the superficial observer, provided evidence of a successful regime only served to increase the hostility of Herod's own subjects on whom the financial burden fell. Jericho and Samaria (now called "Sebaste" in honour of the "adorable" Emperor) were magnificently rebuilt. The new town of Cæsarea rose on the Mediterranean coast, and pagan temples in the Greek cities of the seaboard and of the Decapolis. Jerusalem was not neglected. Its walls were restored on a grand scale and the rebuilding of the Temple itself was begun in 20–19 B.C. The Temple was Herod's *chef-d'œuvre* and its pillared porticos breathed the spirit of Greek art that betrayed the Hellenism of its founder. The inner sanctuary was ready for use within ten years, but the whole work took eighty years to complete; it was finished in A.D. 63, seven years before its final destruction!

The Jews were not placated. The air was heavy with hostility and not even Herod could live and be sane in such an atmosphere. Any opponent, actual or possible, real or imaginary, might beware—particularly the Hasmoneans of whom Herod loved only his wife, Mariamne. Herod's appointment to the High Priesthood of the Hasmonean Aristobulus III was made only under pressure from his mother-in-law, Alexandra. It was a conciliatory move of which Herod soon repented. Aristobulus was too popular and he was drowned in 35 B.C. Herod was suspiciously loud in voicing his regret. The remaining Hasmoneans followed in steady procession. His wife's grandfather, Hyrcanus II, in 30 B.C., Mariamne herself in 29, Alexandra in the following year, his own two children by Mariamne (Alexander and Aristobulus) in 7 B.C., his eldest son (by Doris) five days before his death. Can we wonder at the massacre of a few children in the obscure village of Bethlehem?

IV. After the Death of Herod, 4 B.C.

Herod's last will, subject of course to confirmation by Augustus, divided the territory between his three remaining sons. It named Archelaus king, with Antipas as tetrarch of Galilee and Peræa, and Philip as tetrarch of Trachonitis, Auranitis, Gaulanitis, Batanea and Paneia.

Archelaus was faced with trouble immediately. Herod's death was closely followed by revolt in Jerusalem which Archelaus succeeded in quelling by the massacre of 3,000 Jews. It was a bad beginning. He then set out for Rome whither he was followed by Antipas and by a deputation from the Jewish aristocracy. In his absence the revolt flared up again and spread throughout Palestine. The struggle was particularly fierce in Galilee where Judas, son of Ezechias, had headed the outbreak and taken the town of Sepphoris, one hour's walk from Nazareth. Varus, legate of Syria, destroyed the place and sold all the inhabitants as slaves. Of the Judean insurgents Varus crucified 2,000 in Jerusalem.

Meanwhile in Rome Archelaus and Antipas each pleaded for the kingship, but the Jewish delegation stated its preference for the administrative system of Syria over the rule of Herod's house. None was fully satisfied. Augustus was determined to break what might prove a dangerous unity in Palestine. Archelaus, therefore, became ethnarch, not king, and his territory was the heart of Jewry (Judea, Samaria, Idumea). Antipas and Philip were constituted tetrarchs, independent of Archelaus, of the districts named for them in Herod's will. All three were subject to the legate of Syria.

In Galilee, Antipas (4 B.C.–A.D. 39) was to show more discretion than his brother Archelaus in Judea. He was sensitive to Jewish susceptibilities, building a synagogue in his new city of Tiberias and attending many of the Jewish pilgrimage-feasts. But his adulterous marriage with Herodias, wife of his half-brother Herod-Philip, scandalized Jewish opinion which the Baptist had the fatal courage to voice. Antipas was exiled in A.D. 39, his tetrarchy falling to Agrippa I.

V. Archelaus, 4 b.c.–a.d. 6

Archelaus inherited the vices of his father (cf. Mt. 2. 20). He inherited also an enthusiasm for building, witness the new city of Archelais near Jericho and the restoration of Jericho itself, destroyed in a recent sedition. His tyranny, his arbitary deposition of three successive High Priests and his open contempt for the Law, all combined to send a deputation to Rome asking for his removal. He was deposed by Augustus in the tenth year of his rule and henceforth his territory was governed direct from Rome through the medium of a procurator.

VI. Procuratorial Regime in Judea

Rome had experienced the peculiar delicacy of Judean administration. The problem could scarcely be solved by annexation to the province of Syria since closer supervision and more intimate understanding were necessary. These qualities would not be found in a legate of Syria separated from Judea by the tetrarchy of Antipas and already sufficiently occupied with Syrian affairs. Nor did the size of Judea warrant full provincial status. Augustus, therefore, applied to Judea the special system in vogue for districts of particular administrative difficulty—the procuratorial system.

i. *Religious Situation*

In accordance with its general principles of religious tolerance, Rome granted official recognition to the Jewish faith, centred though it was on the worship of Yahweh in Jerusalem. From the time of Julius Cæsar the Jews were exempt from paying divine homage to the Emperor, though they were bound to him by oath of allegiance since the last days of Herod. The High Priest remained president of the national religion, and twice daily (the custom was introduced by Augustus) sacrifice was offered in the name and at the expense of the Emperor. It was the procurator's duty to see that Jewish religious scruples were respected. Thus, mindful of monotheistic mistrust of images, the Romans refrained (though Pilate twice offended) from bearing their unfurled standards through Jewish territory. For the same reason, the bronze coins minted for common use displayed only floral emblems, though the silver and gold currency bore the image of Cæsar. In common with certain pagan temples in the Empire the Jerusalem Temple enjoyed the right of inviolability, and it was a capital crime for a Gentile to enter its inner court. This prohibition extended to the Roman garrison in the Antonia (the citadel to the north of the Temple).

But the Jewish religion was by no means completely subtracted from Roman supervision since a national religion could be a dangerous force. There was one notable exception to the policy of non-interference, the investiture of the High Priest. Four times during the procuratorship of Valerius Gratus (A.D. 15–26) the right of deposition was exercised. Thus successively were deposed the High Priests Ananos ("Annas", A.D. 6–15), Ismael (in A.D. 16), Eleazar (in 17), Simon (in 18). The last was replaced by Joseph Caiaphas (18–36). The Romans symbolized this control for the thirty years that followed the death of Herod by detaining the vestments of the High Priest in the Antonia. At the time of the great feasts permission was to be sought for their removal, and at these times also Roman soldiers stood on guard in the porticos of the Temple.

ii. *Military Situation*

Unlike the "legatus pro prætore" of Syria, who had his three legions, the Roman procurator in Judea had at his service only cohorts of auxiliaries. These consisted each of one thousand infantry (not five hundred as in the cohorts of a legion), reinforced by a wing or wings of cavalry; they were subdivided into "centuries". In Judea there were five such cohorts; one was stationed in the Antonia at Jerusalem, the majority of the others at Cæsarea Palestinæ, residence of the procurator. Small detachments manned the Herodian fortresses throughout the country. The auxiliaries were in great part Samaritans since the Jews insisted on the exemption from military service expressly granted by Julius Cæsar to accommodate their sabbath and food scruples. Herein, it may be noted, is the seed of future trouble since the Samaritan was the hereditary enemy of the Jew.

In cases of major difficulty appeal would be made to the legate of Syria for military assistance, and in this sense Judea was dependent upon Syria as the Jewish delegation after Herod's death had requested. The legate could also intervene at his own discretion, though without the right to depose the procurator.

The procurator's independence was, in practice, absolute. He was removable by the Emperor alone and Tiberius (A.D. 14–37) favoured a long tenure for his ministers abroad. From his permanent residence at Cæsarea Palestinæ the procurator visited Jerusalem with a powerful escort at the time of the great feasts when excitement might lead to insurrection. There he set up his pretorium either in the former palace of Herod or in the Antonia.

iii. *Juridical and Financial Situation*

The authority of the Jewish supreme court, the Sanhedrin, was respected by the procurator and its decisions had force of law throughout Jewish territory. The administration of justice, too, was in its hands, although, since the power of the procurator was absolute, the execution of capital sentence was not permitted without the ratification of that sentence by the procurator.

Financially the Jews were in no better case than they had been under Herod's administration. The direct taxation, in the form of poll-tax and land-tax, was carefully checked by means of a census recurring every fourteen years. Indirect taxation in the form of purchase-tax and customs duties was collected by officials who were often natives of the country. Under the Empire, rights of customs were auctioned, the actual collection of the duties and taxes being made by "publicans". The publicans aggravated by injustice the natural hostility of the people towards the servants of the oppressor-Power.

iv. *Revolt under the First Procurator*, A.D. 7

Coponius (A.D. 6–9) no sooner reached Palestine than he was faced with revolt. Quirinius, now legate in Syria for the second time, had received orders to make a provincial census.[1] Its application to Judea was the signal for a general rising there under Judas the Galilean. He and his followers resented this open rebuke to their independent nationalism, especially as it was the prelude to financial exactions. They held it a national and religious disgrace to pay tribute to Cæsar. The revolt, though quickly suppressed, betrayed the national feeling which was to simmer for sixty years until it boiled over in the last fatal rebellion of the Jewish people.

v. *Pontius Pilate: Fifth Procurator*, A.D. 26–36

Profane history more than endorses the Gospel impression of Pilate,[2] describing him as cruel, obstinate, arrogant, avaricious. He was at no pains to conciliate his new subjects. When he was yet young in office he deliberately affronted Jewish religious feeling by allowing his troops to march into Jerusalem—into the very Temple precincts, it is said—with

[1] Not to be confused with the census at our Lord's birth.
[2] Though see, besides the Passion story, Lk. 13. 1.

K.P.–I

unfurled banners displaying the portrait of Tiberius Cæsar. On another occasion he publicly exposed to view in the palace of Herod the gilded shields that bore the Emperor's name. This time a petition went to Tiberius who, having reprimanded Pilate, ordered the offending shields to be removed to the temple of Augustus in Cæsarea. Pilate was ultimately deprived of office as a result of an unwarranted attack on a Samaritan gathering at Garizim.

MESSIANIC IDEAS OF THE ROMAN PERIOD

I. THE MESSIAS OF PHARISAISM: THE "PSALMS OF SOLOMON"

We have seen that the Hellenistic period offers little or no evidence of the hope of a Messianic Davidic king, but that the Old Testament promise was not forgotten is apparent from a precious literary survival of the Roman period. This is a collection of eighteen poems on the Biblical model; it is self-styled "The Psalms of Solomon" and is largely of Pharisaic origin. The Pharisees, descendants of the Chasidim of Machabean days, had been bitterly disappointed in the Hasmoneans whose domestic strife had been succeeded by the rule of an idolatrous foreigner. It is therefore no matter for surprise that Pharisaic hopes for the future of Israel should find no place for the Hasmonean dynasty but should turn once more to the traditional Messias of Davidic family. The theme of the seventeenth psalm of this collection is the future establishment of God's Kingdom in Israel by a representative of God ruling in His name. The psalm (dated about 50 B.C.) mirrors the events of the later Hasmonean period: the persecution of the Pharisees by Alexander Jannæus and his foreign mercenaries, the deprival of the Hasmonean dynasty by Pompey. With the throne of Juda vacant (Hyrcanus was ethnarch only), the Pharisees evidently remembered the prophecies which had foretold the recovery of the Davidic house after misfortune and obscurity.[1] This ancient hope now forms the subject of a sublime prayer for the future deliverer, son of David. This prince is to free Jerusalem of its oppressors (v. 22), though not by warlike means (24); he will be wise and just (23) and sinless (35). Though the Chosen of the Lord (32) he is not himself divine since he rules only as God's vicegerent (34). Because this psalm represents the popular Messianic idea of the Gospel period it is worthy of quotation at least in part:

V. 21: "Behold, O Lord, and give them the king the son of David; in Thy chosen time, O God, to rule Thy servant Israel. V. 22: And gird him with strength to subdue the unjust princes; to purge Jerusalem of nations that oppress and destroy. V. 23: Wise and just, let him drive the sinners from the heritage; let him break the pride of sinners like potters' vessels. V. 24: Let him break all their strength with a rod of iron; let him destroy all the lawless nations by the word of his mouth . . . V. 31: Peoples will come from the ends of the earth to see his glory . . . V. 32: He himself is over them as a just king taught of God . . . for all shall be holy and their king, the Messiah (of?) the Lord. V. 34: The Lord himself is their king . . . V. 35: He (the Messiah) shall be free from sin, worthy to rule a great people. V. 37: He shall not fail all his days, leaning upon his God; for God has made him mighty in the spirit of holiness."

It will be noticed that this prayer envisages the establishment *on earth* of the Messianic Kingdom, a notion which derives from the true prophetic tradition. The nature of the earth remains unchanged, but humanity is transformed by the complete triumph of justice and of truth. As for the expected king, he is a man and no more; in other respects, too, he falls short of the Messias of prophecy. "Neither the prophecy of Isaias nor the book of Daniel suggested to the author of the psalm anything surpassing the function of a king and teacher. He (the Messias of these 'Psalms of

[1] E.g. Am. 9. 11.

Solomon') expiates no sin, he addresses no compassionate appeal to lands far off as the Servant of Yahweh had done; he lords it over pagans rather than instructs them."[1] The Messias of the Psalms of Solomon is a pale ghost of the Messias of the Prophets.

II. THE MESSIAS OF THE "ZEALOTS"

Provided the national religion was in no danger the Pharisees were content to wait and pray for the coming of the Davidic king. Others were not so patient, nor were they so particular that their liberator should be of Davidic family. The year of Herod's death (4 B.C.) saw a crop of popular and pugnacious leaders, though the names of only three are known: Judas, son of Ezechias, in Galilee; Simon, once Herod's slave, in Peræa; a certain Anthronges in Judea. Each claimed royalty and each had a considerable following which indicates, doubtless, that the leaders claimed a divine mission of liberation. After the stern suppression of the revolt of a second Judas (Judas "the Galilean") which broke out in Judea in the first days of the procuratorial regime (A.D. 7) these "zealot" Jews were forced to give up the struggle. But they did not despair of the ultimate triumph of what they felt to be God's cause.

III. THE "OTHER-WORLDLY" MESSIAS

While certain of the "Zealots" still cherished the hope of securing God's triumph on earth by force of arms, others succumbed to misfortune and came to despair of this present world. These turned their thoughts and hopes to a new creation built on the ruins of the old, and to a Saviour from on high who would introduce this new age. This new current of Messianic thought is represented in the Jewish apocalyptical writings of the Roman period, notably in the First Book

[1] M.-J. Lagrange, O.P., *Le Judaisme avant Jésus Christ*, p. 385.

of Henoch where the "Son of Man" or the "Elect One" is pre-existent in heaven, already endowed with divine glory though not equal to God. In due time this Being will descend from heaven with the sole purpose of destroying the enemies of God's people. This new conception of the Kingdom and of the King marks a break with prophetic Messianism, for it denies an earthly existence to the Kingdom and an earthly, saving function to the Messiah.

IV. THE MESSIANISM OF QUMRAN

The Dead Sea Scrolls recently discovered (cf. p. 24) have revealed the hopes of a Jewish sect in the first century B.C. This community of Qumran was Essene, a sect already known to history as a group with high religious ideals but withdrawn from the mass of Judaism on which it had no influence. It lived a monastic life of asceticism and religious observance but would have nothing to do with the Temple worship, since it regarded the official priesthood as corrupt. The withdrawal to Qumran took place, with some probability, about 150 B.C.

The admirable religious life of the community's members was designed to "prepare the way of the Lord", to make ready for the great day when God would secure the victory of the Sons of Light over the Sons of Darkness.[1] When the war was over, God would initiate a new era. In this task His instruments, it appears, would be three in number: "the Prophet" who would come first (about him nothing more is known), and then two Messiahs: "the Messiah of Aaron" and "the Messiah of Israel". The Messiah of Aaron was to be High Priest, superior to the Messiah of Israel; he was to be the official interpreter of the Law. The Messiah of Israel was to be of the royal line of David (the "branch" of David,

---

[1] This Holy War was later to be identified by them with the anti-Roman Jewish revolt of A.D. 67–70 which they supported—with fatal results to the community.

cf. Zach. 2. 8 ; 6. 12) he was to be the political leader, no more.

The idea of two Messiahs is strange and the Old Testament has not prepared us for it.[1] Nevertheless, the Davidic, royal, Messiah of the prophets is associated in the Old Testament with the idea of priesthood (cf. p. 53). Qumran, therefore, imagined two Messiahs, one of priestly Levitical descent, the other of royal Judan extraction. Christianity, on the other hand, recognized only one who united priesthood and kingship in himself; our Lord was indeed of Juda and not from Levi, but neither was his priesthood a Levitical one (p. 53), it was by direct conferment of God; he was "a priest after the manner of Melchisedech" (on this, see Heb. 7. 1–19).

---

[1] It should be observed, however, that after the Exile and the extinction of the monarchy the priestly aspect of the future Leader comes to the fore, though the royal aspect does not disappear.

CHAPTER X
THE KINGDOM AWAITS
THE KING

I. MONOTHEISM AND THE LAW

Twice daily the Jew recited the prayer which begins:
"Hear, O Israel, the Lord our God in one Lord", and upon
the word "one", according to the instruction of the Rabbis,
special emphasis was to be laid. All-powerful, Yahweh con-
trols the movements of history; all-holy, He expects the
sanctification of His people; just and merciful, He condemns
sin but seeks the conversion of the sinner. By supreme right
of creation Yahweh was God of all the nations, but He had
chosen Israel to be the recipient of His constantly growing
revelation and its custodian.

The expression of God's will for His people was the
"Torah", the inspired Mosaic code contained in the first
five books of the Sacred Writings. This body of laws
dominated religious life and formed the spiritual bond which
united all Jews at home and abroad. Upon its observance
depended the fulfilment of God's promises to the nation.
Loyalty to God's Law was an infallible means of pleasing
Him for it meant the recognition of His sovereign rights—
it meant the "kingship of God".

This devotion was admirable and was shared by Jesus
himself, but it had its dangers. Many problems had arisen
from the application of the Law to individual cases and the
traditional solutions of these problems had been carefully
listed by the Scribes. A multitude of minute regulations,
almost impossible of observance, had thus grown up around
the Law. The ceremonial precepts, too, came in the course
of time to receive equal emphasis with the moral commands,
and the letter of their fulfilment tended to absorb the spirit

of true piety before it reached the depths of the soul. This tendency was most marked in Pharisaic circles. In practice it led to an insistence on outward acts which in its turn might easily lead to hypocrisy. In effect this hypocrisy was neither inevitable nor universal, but it was sufficiently common to earn the lament of the Jews in Christian times and the severe rebukes of our Lord himself (Mt. 23. 1–36).

Amongst the simple folk of the countryside the village synagogue did valuable work. Prayer, readings from the Law and from the Prophets, together with an explanatory homily, took place on Sabbaths and feast-days. Sacrifice was, of course, reserved to the Temple in Jerusalem. The influence of the synagogue was deep and widespread; it produced fruits of sound piety among the Jews and, among the Gentiles, the knowledge of monotheism which was to help the Apostles in their work.

II. MESSIANISM

I. THE KINGDOM

The monotheistic belief together with devotion to the Mosaic Law combined to give shape to Israel's singular confidence in the future. The day would come ("the Day of Yahweh") when the One God would assert His universal rights at last; this day would see the destruction of those who opposed His sovereignty and the beginning of a new era of happiness. This new period of world-history would see the widespread acknowledgment of the Torah, God's expressed will for human conduct. The adoption of Israel's Law by all the nations would naturally mean that Israel would be held in universal honour.[1]

---

[1] Past history and the divine promises had shown that whereas infidelity had brought the overthrow of the Davidic kingdom, faithfulness to Yahweh's Law had always meant political prosperity. It was therefore to be expected that the new era of religious fervour would mean *political* domination of the world by the chosen People. We are consequently not surprised when we find that the Jewish outlook, while not entirely ignoring the spiritual prosperity of the future age, grows by little and little more material.

What place were the Gentiles to hold in the Kingdom? Not only the prophets[1] but even the earliest promises (e.g. Gen. 12. 3) had made it clear that God intended to work the salvation of all the world. This belief was faithfully preserved amongst the best in Israel (e.g. Simeon; cf. Lk. 2. 30–32). But the last centuries before Christ had brought a change: Israel's unfortunate experiences at the hands of the pagans had succeeded in distorting the original idea of the destiny of paganism. In the general opinion of Jewry the great mass of the Gentiles were destined for final destruction in "the world to come". This fate could be averted by the acceptance of circumcision with the whole obligation of the Law or even, as it seems, by a renunciation of idolatrous worship.[2] Such as these would receive a place, though an inferior one, even in the Messianic kingdom on earth.

We have drawn a distinction between the Messianic kingdom on earth and "the world to come", and this is the opinion which is more in line with prophetic tradition and which so prevailed that we may call it the "orthodox" opinion; we find it uppermost in the Gospel story. In this view, the Messianic kingdom was to be an intermediary period of Jewish political and religious supremacy. It would end (after 40? 1,000? 7,000? years) with the final judgment, the resurrection of the dead, the "world to come". Nevertheless, a different conception of the Kingdom of God is found, as we have seen,[3] in much of the Jewish apocalyptic literature during and after the first two centuries which preceded the coming of our Lord. This second view,

---

[1] Cf. especially the second half of Isaias' prophecy.

[2] Those who accepted circumcision with its obligations were full converts ("proselytes of Justice"); they were a very small minority. The great majority of converted pagans did not accept circumcision but, having abjured their idolatry, were allowed to take part in synagogue-worship. These "fearers of God" were the recipients, with the Jews, of the early Christian preaching (Ac. 13. 16) and great numbers of them believed (Ac. 13. 43).

[3] P. 122.

despairing of the present world, places its hopes entirely in "the world to come" and the prospect of a Messianic kingdom on earth disappears completely; the "Day of Yahweh" is not the day when the Messias goes forth to his earthly triumph but the day of the world's end and of the final judgment of which the Messias is merely the herald.

Each of these two schools of thought sacrificed something of the Messianic message which the prophets had faithfully delivered. The first made too sharp a distinction between the Messianic kingdom and "the world to come"; it failed to see that the Kingdom was to be a period of spiritual blessings offered as a preparation for "the world to come". The second school went to the opposite extreme and lost sight altogether of the new spiritual opportunities which would be presented in a new spiritual kingdom on earth. The truth lay between the two notions. The Kingdom on earth and "the world to come" were simply two stages of the one great reality—the Kingdom of God; the first was to be the preparatory stage, the second was to be the Kingdom in its perfect and final form. It was our Lord who brought together the elements of truth in the two conflicting theories, and in doing so He showed the ultimate unity of the earthly and heavenly kingdom, embracing both in one phrase: the Kingdom of God.

II. THE KING

What conclusion did our Lord's contemporaries draw from the various prophecies of the future King? It must be noted at once that they failed to unite in one picture the partial sketches handed down by the prophets. This is scarcely surprising—the Jews could not grasp the idea of a glorious king who was to suffer and die. And yet Judaism is to be blamed. Despite the apparent contradictions, there was no excuse for sacrificing any of the outlines of the prophetic picture; had these been faithfully preserved, Judaism might have been prepared to recognize the Messias when he came. Instead of a complete picture we find that the outline of a suffering Messias has disappeared; we find also that, as in the case of the Kingdom, two schools of thought hold opposed views of the King. The Messianism of the Psalms of Solomon[1] makes the Messias a man and no more, but the Messias of the Book of Henoch is a mysterious Being from heaven who, it seems, was already in existence before the world was made. Again each of these views has something of truth in it in so far as each reflects one side of the prophetic tradition; again our Lord resolves the apparent contradiction, this time in His own Person. Because He possessed a twofold nature, one human the other divine, He could tell the Jews that though they knew His origin yet they knew it not (Jn. 7. 28).

i. *The Davidic Messias and His Work*

Though for a time the figure of a Davidic king had been allowed to fall into the background,[2] it was impossible for long to ignore the prophecies which were perfectly clear on this point. The title "Son of David", therefore, became the most popular term for the Messias; we find it on the lips of the people (Mt. 12. 23; 21. 9) and in His argument with the Pharisees (Mk. 12. 35–37), our Lord takes for granted the Davidic sonship of the Messias.

It was the belief of some that the Messias would be born in Bethlehem, David's town. This at least was the conviction of Herod's Jewish advisers (Mt. 2. 5) and of others (Jn. 7. 42). Yet his origin was to be in some way obscure since the people make it an objection to our Lord's Messianity that they knew (or thought they knew) His parents (Jn. 6. 42). The solemn manifestation of the Messias, when it came, would be sudden

---

[1] Cf. p. 132.
[2] In the early days of the Hasmoneans; cf. p. 106 f.

and surprising;[1] it would be preceded, too, by the coming
of Elias in person—hence the question put to the Baptist
(Jn. 1. 21), the doubt of the Apostles (Mk. 9. 10), the gibe
offered to our Lord on the Cross (Mk. 15. 36).

We have seen that the Messias of popular Jewish belief
was to be a political Messias, lieutenant of Yahweh, conqueror and vicegerent of the earthly Golden Age ("the Days
of the Messias"). But the spiritual benefits of that Age were
to be the result of the direct action of Yahweh Himself while
the Messias was merely to remove the political obstacles
that were in the way. The Messias could not forgive sins, for
example; only God could do that (Mk. 2. 7). Much less
could he expiate those sins by a sacrificial death—Peter had
never been instructed thus in his synagogue (Mk. 8. 32).
The Messias could not alter the inviolable Law of Yahweh;
he was not lord, for instance, of the Sabbath (Mk. 2. 28).
Nor was he to judge humanity; even the "transcendent"
Messias of the Jewish apocalypses was no more than a herald
of God's judgment. In neither school of thought, as we have
seen, was the Messias regarded as actually achieving the
salvation of the individual soul in "the world to come." This
wholesale denial of spiritual privilege to the Messias was not
warranted by prophetic tradition rightly interpreted and
sharply contradicted our Lord's own claims. His mission was,
as we shall see,[2] profoundly spiritual and the eternal destiny
of each soul was to depend on its attitude to Him who was
to come as Judge (Mk. 8. 38).

ii. *The Divinity of the Messias*

Despite prophetic indications the Jews did not await a
Messias of divine origin. When, for instance, Yahweh
addressed the Messias as His "son" (e.g. Ps. 2. 7), the Jews

---

[1] Perhaps this is the motive that lies behind the temptation of Lk. 4.
9–12.

[2] See the following chapter.

saw no more in the expression than a guarantee of special divine favour. This does not mean, however, that the Jewish mind was entirely unprepared for our Lord's revelation of His divinity. Though there were few, there must certainly have been some who penetrated more deeply into the sacred prophecies and who could appreciate the revelation when it came. Moreover much of the Jewish literature before Christ endows the Messias with such gifts of infallibility and even of omnipotence that we begin to wonder how the figure of a merely political Messias could have remained at all. The "apocalyptic" literature withdraws the Messianic figure still further from human nature and shrouds his image in mystery.

iii. *The Sufferings of the Messias*

The notion of a suffering Messias was quite at variance with Jewish national hopes. The difficulty of the Isaian passages which speak of the Messias' passion and death was surmounted in one of two ways: either by making the prophet refer to the sufferings of the whole nation of Israel or by adjusting the text itself while still applying it to the Messias. Thus, for example, the sentence: "He shall be led as a sheep to the slaughter" becomes "He shall lead the nations to the slaughter".[1] Conscientious meditation on the prophecies might have revealed their true meaning and evidently did so in some cases,[2] but the mass of the ordinary folk, amongst whom we must count the Apostles, would look to their unenlightened leaders for interpretation.

It is interesting that the Judaism of Christian times was forced to yield some ground in this dispute. It sought to explain the Isaian passion prophecies by inventing a "Messias, son of Joseph"[3] who was to prepare the way for the "Messias,

---

[1] Cf. Is. 53. 7 as rendered in an Aramaic paraphrase of the second century A.D.

[2] In Simeon's, for example (Lk. 1. 34, 35).

[3] I.e. descended not from Juda but from the patriarch Joseph.

son of David". The former would suffer and die, for the second death was unthinkable, but he might suffer before his kingdom was successfully established.

III. THE TITLES USED BY OUR LORD
I. SON OF MAN

This strange expression seems to have slipped into the common speech from Hebrew poetic use (e.g. Ps. 8. 5) where it evidently meant simply "a man-child", "a man", with some emphasis on man's lowly nature in comparison, for example, with God. Hence the phrase, *of itself*, does not designate the Messias. In the book of Daniel, however (Dan. 7. 13), "one like a son of man" comes on the clouds to receive power and majesty from Yahweh. It is clear from the context that this figure symbolizes the Messias, king of the Messianic kingdom. The term "son of man" therefore, though a general one, could be made pointedly Messianic by an open reference to Daniel's prophecy. For these reasons it served our Lord's purpose well. Without inopportunely proclaiming His Messiahship to the ordinary people He could use the phrase in reference to Himself when He wished to emphasize His humanity. Yet the very strangeness and repetition of the term[1] seem to have been designed to attract attention, and when the time came for clear speaking the same phrase was used again. Challenged by the High Priest our Lord presented Himself as "the son of man sitting on the right hand of the power of God and coming with the clouds of heaven" (Mk. 14. 62). Surrounded thus with the circumstances of Daniel's vision, the long familiar phrase now stood out in all its Messianic meaning. This is but another example of the divine prudence of our Lord's revelation. The best lessons are those which have not to be at any time unlearnt but which are capable of an evergrowing understanding.

[1] It occurs in Mk. 2. 10; 2. 28; 8. 31; 8. 38; 9. 8; 9. 11; 9. 30; 10. 33; 10. 45; 13. 26; 14. 21; 14. 41; 14. 62.

II. Son of God

The expression as its stands was not a synonym for the Messias in Jewish literature, though it was eminently suitable of application to the Messias since every just man is regarded in Hebrew thought as a "son of God". Our Lord, therefore, could use the phrase without shocking the well-disposed and yet without openly declaring His Messiahship. Moreover, the expression lent itself to the possibility of a continually deepening meaning, a meaning which our Lord intended ultimately to give to it. Clearly the phrase is capable of breaking the boundaries of "adoptive" sonship—the sonship of the just man—and of emerging into the "natural" Sonship of God which our Lord claimed for Himself. That this Sonship of His was of a kind quite different from that of the just man is apparent from all the divine characteristics with which He surrounds His use of the title.

IV. THE PHARISEES: THEIR ATTITUDE TO THE MESSIAS

The Pharisees appear in the Gospels as the promoters and leaders of the opposition to Jesus. Who were they?

The name "Pharisee" ("separatist" in the religious, and probably also in the political, sense) appears for the first time during the reign of John Hyrcanus (135–104 B.C.), but the roots of the party are to be found in the "Chasidim" of Machabean days (1 Mac. 2. 27).[1] They were the natural allies of the Machabees and of their descendants the Hasmoneans, but they became bitterly opposed to the union of sovereignty and high priesthood in the person of Jonathan (153 B.C.). The opposition came to a head under John Hyrcanus who thereupon lent his support to the Sadducees.[2] The Pharisees

[1] See p. 93.
[2] A party recruited largely from the Jewish nobility; it grouped itself about the High Priest and to it the High Priest normally belonged. Its influence with the people was fortunately negligible for its faith was corrupted by materialism, denying—as it did—the resurrection of the body and the immortality of the soul.

returned to favour under Alexandra (76–67 B.C.) when their decisions received the force of law. Having refused the oath of allegiance to the foreigner Herod, they retired from politics and devoted themselves to religious affairs. In this sphere their authority was acknowledged, though not strictly official—the full legal authority still lay with the High Priest and his council (the "Sanhedrin"). It was the influence of the Pharisees with the people which made their minority membership of this council such a powerful one.

The Messianic opinions of Pharisaism we have already seen in the Psalms of Solomon, and indeed they are written on the pages of the Gospels because the opinions of the people were the opinions of their respected instructors, the Pharisees. The Messianic policy of Pharisaism steered a middle course between that of the Zealots on the one hand and that of the Sadducees on the other. The Zealots were for warlike action against Rome, wholehearted submission suited the Sadducees who thrived on the existing state of affairs; the Zealots looked too eagerly for a Messias, the Sadducees preferred to forget him. Meanwhile the Pharisees waited. They did not renounce their Messianic hopes of a restoration of national independence, but they counselled for the time being a prudent submission to the ruling power.

Why were the Pharisees so hostile to our Lord? The reason is not to be found in His claim to Messiahship because this was not made clearly and publicly until the end of His life, whereas Pharisaic opposition was already bitter in the first days of the Public Ministry (cf. Mk. 2.1—3.6). The cause of their antagonism was twofold and betrayed their misunderstanding of both Kingdom and King.

In the first place, our Lord's religious viewpoint was quite other than the Pharisaic ideal. The Pharisees must quickly have recognized that Jesus sought what was in fact a higher and deeper sanctity than their own; this new holiness threatened their monopoly of professional sanctity because it was offered to Law-learned and ignorant alike. Nor had the new Teacher even consulted the Pharisees; it seemed that their assumed authority was being usurped. Moreover, the principles laid down by Jesus, if carried to their logical conclusions, would open the gate not only to all classes in Israel, including the despised multitude, but even to all nations. The shrewd Pharisee must have asked himself what was to become of the Jewish religion as a proud national possession.

It is likely, however, that this was not the full reason for their hostility. Had Jesus been content with the infusion of a new spirit into Legal observance it is not unlikely that many of the Pharisees would simply have asked for His credentials, and these credentials, in the form of miracles, abounded. But our Lord's claim evidently went much further. He did not claim to be but another prophet in the long line of prophets, rather He presented Himself as a being apart with the privileges of God Himself. Monotheism was shocked. The Pharisees, confident that they possessed the fullness of revelation, would wait for no explanations; they preferred to ignore or to explain away the manifestly divine guarantees which the new Teacher had to offer. This was their crime.

V. MESSIANISM IN THE DIASPORA

I. THE JEWS OF THE DISPERSION

The tide of exile and of emigration had brought Palestinian Jews to Mesopotamia, Syria, Egypt, Greece and Italy. As they spread they multiplied; it is calculated, for instance, that in the first century after Christ the half-million population of Alexandria included two hundred thousand Jews. Throughout the Empire they established themselves in compact communities whose religious and civil independence was guaranteed by Roman law. Jerusalem, however, remained their religious centre,[1] and thither they sent their offerings and a multitude of pilgrims yearly for the feast of the Pasch. They adopted the Greek language of their new homes and used it in the synagogues to preserve and to propagate their ancestral religion.

Nationalistic sentiment was naturally not as strong among the Jews of the Dispersion (the "Diaspora") as it was in Palestine and it lacked the stimulus of political oppression. We are not therefore surprised to find that the Messianic hope languished among the emigrés. Certainly the Alexandrian translators of the Old Testament did not attempt to force Messianic interpretations into passages which did not already contain them.

II. PHILO

Philo, the Jewish genius of Alexandria (? 30 B.C.–A.D. 42), found little room for political Messianism in his philosophy. Philo was concerned rather with the morality of individual souls than with the future glory of the Israelitic nation. Writing for Jews surrounded by Greek thought he aimed at combining all that was best in Greek moral philosophy with the sure truths of Jewish revelation, particularly as they are contained in the five books of Moses. This he sought to achieve by freely applying allegorical interpretation to the books of Moses.[2] Philo, therefore, though a strict Jew, was not narrow in his outlook. For him, indeed, the Mosaic Law was paramount, but he looked forward to the day when its

---

[1] The half-schismatic temple of Leontopolis in Egypt (to the northeast of Heliopolis) does not appear to have attracted the loyalty of the Alexandrian Jews. It was founded about 170 B.C. by Onias IV, the refugee son of the murdered High Priest Onias III (cf. p. 92).

[2] For example: in the story of the Fall (Gen. 2.25—3.7) Adam represents the human "mind", Eve the "senses"; the serpent is "pleasure" which appeals first to the senses and through them allures the mind from God. Note, however, that Philo did not deny the historical truth of the story but *added* an allegorical explanation.

excellence would be acknowledged and its practice observed by all nations.

In this sense we may certainly speak of Philo's "Messianism", if we understand that term in its widest possible significance. It was a genuine Israelitic Messianism, too, because world-wide recognition of the Law would inevitably redound to Israel's glory. But did Philo nurse also the hope of an individual who would produce this desirable state of affairs? In other words, may we speak of Philo's "Messianism" in the strict sense?

This hope was assuredly not bound up with Philo's philosophical system. On the contrary, he maintained that the Law had sufficient divine weight of itself to make its excellence universally felt. Yet there are a few passages in Philo's more nationalistic writings in which he betrays the hope of a divinely-sent hero. This figure would establish concord among all nations, by force if necessary, and would rule in peace a world-kingdom founded by God. It is characteristic of Philo, the citizen of the world, that he does not assert the Israelitic origin of the hero; indeed when he paints the future age in the colours of Isaian Messianism (Is. 11. 6) he omits all mention of the king sprung from Davidic stock (Is. 11. 1, 10).

It will be noticed that Philo was nearer to the Christian truth than the Pharisees were. His concern for the well-being of the individual soul led him to hope for a liberation which was above all spiritual. Yet his rigid monotheism would have rebelled against the suggestion that the Liberator was to be the incarnate Son of God.

CHAPTER XI
THE KING IN PERSON[1]
I. HIS MOTHER

In the days of the monarchy an official position at Juda's court was held by the *gebirah* or Great Lady. She was the queen-mother and her office, as it seems, dated from the day of her son's coronation, though it did not cease with his death. The first to hold this office in Juda was Solomon's mother, Bathsheba, who sat at her son's right hand (3 Kg. 2. 19).[2] The importance of this function is emphasized by the fact that in the books of 3 and 4 Kings all but three of the kings are introduced with a mention of the mother's name. In the royal messianism of Isaias and Micheas (pp. 61–64) we have already seen very pointed reference to the mother of the future king. It may be that we have some explanation of this in the institution of the *gebirah*.

The New Testament speaks very plainly. When Elizabeth meets Mary she exclaims: "Whence is this to me that the mother of my lord (i.e. of my lord the king) should come to me?" (Lk. 1. 43). Evidently Elizabeth recognized here a dignity that was Mary's own, though her own by reason of her son-to-be. She had good reason. The angel had already approached Mary with the message that she was to be mother of one to whom God would give "the throne of David his father" (Lk. 1. 32); the name Mary was now to be written in the annals of the kings of Juda. But unlike the queen-mother of the old kingdom, she is not merely named, she is presented as a person of interest in her own right, and when we have read the first two chapters of Luke's gospel

---

[1] For the order of events taken as a basis for this chapter confer the "Additional Note" at the end.

[2] Cf. R. de Vaux, Les Institutions de l'Ancien Testament, vol. 1, 1958, pp. 180–182.

we feel we know her well. The surprising influence of this queen-mother with her son is described in the second chapter of the gospel of St John: the evangelist gives us the clear impression that Mary persists despite her son's reluctance, and that her persistence (like that of another woman, Mt. 15. 21–28) wins the day (Jn. 2. 1–12). With Mary, therefore, our Lord's public life began and with Mary it ended. She had learned by hard experience that he had to leave her to be "about his Father's work" (Lk. 2. 49), that he could call "mother" only the one who heard the word of God and practised it (Lk. 8. 21), but she had already said "Be it done to me according to thy word" (Lk. 1. 38) and had "kept these words in her heart" (Lk. 1. 51). It was not surprising that a mother, a queen-mother, so constant stood by her son's Cross (Jn. 19. 25 ff.), the strange throne of the "greater than Solomon" (Mt. 12. 42), or that after his death she should be found with the Twelve (Ac. 1. 14).

At the beginning of the third century Origen was already writing: "Since the Christian himself lives no longer but Christ lives in him, the words apply to him that were spoken to Mary: Behold thy son" (Jn. 19. 26). Origen was drawing attention to the power of the queen-mother, not broken but enhanced by the son's death, and to the claim the Christian has upon it.

II. HIS BIRTH

The prophet Micheas had promised great things for the little village of Bethlehem (Mal. 5. 1–4). Seven hundred years later a child was born there in obscurity. Mary and Joseph knew that the child had no human father (Lk. 1. 34 f.; Mt. 1. 18–20)—he was virgin-born (cf. Is. 7. 14). Strange as it seemed, they knew that he was to occupy the Davidic throne for ever (Lk. 1. 32 f.; cf. 2 Kg. 7. 11–16) and to achieve not a political conquest but a spiritual one (Mt. 1. 21; Lk. 1. 72 f.). In him all the nations of the earth were to be blessed because he had been sent by a God mindful of His promise to Abraham (Gen. 22. 7); this Mary knew (Lk. 1. 55) and Zachary, father of the Baptist (Lk. 1. 72 f.). Since the conquest was to be the spiritual thing so constantly emphasized by the prophets, it was clear from the outset that disappointment awaited those who looked first for a national deliverance. Simeon, therefore, when the child was six weeks old, foresaw opposition from Israel itself (Lk. 2. 34) as Isaias had hinted long before (Is. 53. 8 f.). Yet Israel was not the whole object of the child's mission for he was destined to be the light of paganism (Lk. 2. 32; cf. Is. 49. 6).

In short, the little circle surrounding the child was firmly convinced that Messianic days had come at last; Mary and Joseph instructed by the angel, Elizabeth (Lk. 1. 42), Zachary (Lk. 1. 65–79), Simeon (Lk. 2. 25 f.) and Anna (Lk. 2. 36–38) all enlightened by God, saw in the child the Expectation of Israel. But when this title was to be urged before a wider public unprivileged with an immediate revelation from God, it became necessary to furnish evidence. If the prophecies meant anything at all, and to a Jew they meant everything, a claimant to Messiahship must first establish his Davidic descent. Neither St Luke (3. 23–38) nor St Matthew (1. 1–17) could afford to ignore this demand. Indeed, St Matthew, thinking of his Jewish readers, felt compelled to place the documented proof at the head of his Gospel; after this necessary introduction he could then allow the events to speak for themselves.[1]

III. HIS HERALD

When the child became a man He was introduced to the world by John, the son of Zachary, who had sought to make

---

[1] It seems most probable that both genealogies are Joseph's and that Luke traces Joseph's line not by way of physical descent but by way of juridical ancestry recognized in Jewish Law (perhaps as in Lk. 20. 28; cf. Deut. 25. 5). As for our Lord's Davidic origin, He possessed it legally through His foster-father but physically through His virgin-Mother who, as St Luke gives us to understand (Lk. 1. 32, 69) was actually of David's family.

Israel worthy of His coming (Mk. 1. 3 f.). On his own admission (Jn. 1. 23) the Baptist was no more than a herald making ready for a greater than himself (Jn. 1. 27). Yet John's own office was not without honour for, as his father knew, he was Prophet of the Highest (Lk. 1. 76) and the Messias was to pronounce him the greatest figure of the Old Dispensation (Lk. 7. 28). He had found a place, too, in the prophetic vision of Messianic days:

"Behold I send my messenger to make clear the path before Me; and straightway there shall come to his temple the Lord whom ye seek and the Angel of the Alliance whom ye desire . . . Behold I send to you Elias the prophet before the day of Yahweh, great and terrible, shall come!" (Mal. 3. 1, 4, 5.)

A second Moses, mediator of a new alliance, was to be preceded by a messenger who would prepare hearts for the great day of His coming (Mal. 4. 6). The Baptist was a voice in Israel (Mk. 1. 3), like the voice heard by the prophet Isaias (Is. 40. 3), but this time the voice announced and prepared a greater, more deeply spiritual recovery than Zorobabel, the Davidic prince, could ever have brought.

Yet Malachy had called the messenger "Elias" and the Scribes had found no deeper meaning when they expounded the text in the synagogues. The Apostles, therefore, were puzzled when Elias appeared at the Transfiguration only to disappear again (Mk. 9. 2–13). It was left to our Lord to explain the profounder meaning of Malachy's sentence. Side by side with the great Lawgiver, Elias came as the great champion of the pure religion of Israel[1] to show that Jesus was his Master in the same cause. But the "Elias" who was to come before the great day of Yahweh had already done his work. Malachy had not spoken[2] of Elias in the flesh but of one who would work as ardently as Elias had done for the

[1] Cf. 3 Kg. cc. 18–21.
[2] It is possible, though not necessary, to suppose that in Mk. 9. 12 our Lord concedes the reappearance of Elias in the flesh before the Last Day and Second Coming of the Messias.

true cause of Yahweh, of an Elias "in spirit". This was the
Baptist of whom the angel had said: He shall go before the
Lord in the spirit and power of Elias (Lk. 1. 17).

IV. HIS MESSAGE

A. JESUS THE TEACHER-MESSIAS

The prophets had foretold an age when the knowledge of
God would be more perfect and more profound than in their
own time (Jer. 31. 31–34; Is. 54. 13). The fortunate people
of this period were to be instructed by God himself through
the medium of a Messias-Counsellor (Is. 9. 6) in whom was
to be the spirit of God's own wisdom (Is. 11. 2). His weapon
of war was to be his doctrine: he was to "strike the earth with
the rod of his mouth" (Is. 11. 4).

If somewhat obscured by their hopes of a material kingdom
the idea still remained fixed in Jewish minds. Thus "the rod
of his mouth" finds an echo in the "Psalms of Solomon"
(17. 24), and the Samaritan woman expects a Messias "who
will tell us all things" (Jn. 4. 25). So also the Galileans style
the Messias "the prophet" (i.e. the teacher from God) "who
is to come" (Jn. 6. 14), while many in Jerusalem are led by
the force of our Lord's doctrine to say "this is the Messias"
(Jn. 7. 40–41).

This teacher to come would be characterized by the gentle
prudence of his revelation, yet his doctrine would be com-
pelling and would enlighten not only Jews but pagans also
(Is. 42. 1–7).

In this, as in all other respects, Jesus more than fulfils the
prophecies; they are the outline, He is the finished portrait;
He is the substance of which they are the shadow; He completes their incompleteness and explains by His person and
by His work the full import of the prophetic message which
even the prophets themselves, in all probability, could not
hope to appreciate.

i. *The Problem before Jesus*

Our Lord did not claim to be a revolutionary. His new revelation was to draw nourishment from the soil of Judaism in which it was to be sown. There were three elements in that soil which could nourish the seed. First, monotheism which divided the Jews sharply from their idolatrous neighbours and masters. Second, Messianism: the Jews were confident in their glorious future which was to be secured by a king of Davidic birth. Third, a sincere devotion to the Mosaic Law; this devotion manifested itself in public acts or worship, regularly performed, and in practical charity towards their fellow Jew.

Each of these elements could be used in the new revelation, indeed that was the divinely planned reason for their very existence, but each had first to be freed of the human defects which had gathered about it. Of the three, the monotheistic belief alone had resisted the test of time, though even here there was a rigidity which might refuse to bend before the revelation of three Persons in one God. The Messianic hope had become material and selfishly national; it had forgotten that the Messias was to be not only "the glory of his people, Israel" but also "a light to the revelation of the Gentiles" (Lk. 2. 32). The divine Law itself, through undue preoccupation with its external demands and with the Pharisaic observances which surrounded them, had begun to sap the strength of true interior piety.

Our Lord therefore was confronted with a threefold problem: how to turn exterior piety inwards; how to spiritualize and universalize the Messianic outlook; how to reveal the divinity of His own person without striking a mortal blow at Jewish monotheism. Each of these difficulties called for its own solution. Our Lord's solution will be examined under the separate headings of His Moral Teaching, His Redemptive Death, His Revelation of His

Divinity. But there are certain characteristics which underlie
all His teaching and which we may call His General Method.

ii. *General Method of Jesus*

In the first place our Lord sought to draw the Jews by
means of His own supremely winning personality. He was
Himself sinless (Jn. 8. 46) yet "the friend of sinners"
(Lk. 7. 34); willing to undergo hardship (Lk. 9. 58), unwilling to inflict it unnecessarily upon others (Mk. 8. 2–3)
and full of practical sympathy for the sick and bereaved
(Mt. 14. 14; Lk. 7. 15). Yet with the affection of His nature
there went an air of unmistakable authority which lent a
quiet assurance to His teaching (Mk. 1. 22) and a fearlessness
to His denunciation of proud oppressors (Mt. 23. 13–36).

But it is not enough that the personality of the teacher
should be attractive, his lesson, too, must be interesting and
stimulating. Our Lord therefore used vivid pictures which
were either traditional (like the Shepherd; Jn. 10. 11–18;
cf. Ez. c. 34), or familiar (like the agricultural and fishing
images; Mt. 6. 28–29), or attractive for their own sake (like
the little children; Lk. 18. 15–17). To rouse His audience
and to stimulate them to reflect upon His teaching He used
the parable method of instruction which though sown in
the mind almost unnoticed would remain there to grow into
great understanding if only the soil had the necessary
qualities (e.g. Mt. 13. 1–35).

Above all He threw into high relief the loving Fatherhood
of God (Lk. 12. 6–7). To make even the path of renunciation
attractive He stressed the positive love for a Father rather
than the less fruitful fear of a Taskmaster. God must be
feared, but before all He must be loved.

iii. *The Moral Teaching of Jesus*

For fifteen hundred years the inspired Mosaic Law had

preserved ideals of justice in the Jewish nation and the knowledge of God in the world. In what sense did its moral
teaching need to be "fulfilled" by Christ (Mt. 5. 17)?

The Law had not neglected the hidden intentions of the
heart (Deut. 6. 5), but as a national code designed for a
people in process of spiritual formation it had laid stress on
man's outward actions. This emphasis should naturally have
been corrected with spiritual progress, and the prophets had
laboured to this end (e.g. Os. 6. 6), but the Pharisees were
undoing their work. Our Lord saw the danger. He accordingly made it clear (Mk. 12. 30) that of all the commandments of the Law the most important is the love of God.
This must be the prevailing motive of thought and action—
not the love of self, which is complacent (Lk. 17. 10), nor
the desire to attract the attention of others (Mt. 6. 16–18).
If God is adored in spirit and in truth (Jn. 4. 23) the appro-
priate external acts will follow. Convinced of the Fatherhood
of God, the whole man with his inmost thoughts will devote
himself to God and accordingly his holiness "will abound
more than that of the Pharisees" (Mt. 5. 20).

In this way, our Lord's teaching goes down to the roots
of vice and of virtue. Not only murder and adultery but the
hate and the impure desire which feed them must be
pitilessly cut out (Mt. 5. 21 f.). It is in the same profound
spirit that He pronounces the blessedness of the obscurity
which comes from humility, self-forgetfulness, self-efface-
ment (Mt. 5. 3–12). These are the virtues of little showing
which earn the Kingdom, for the New Covenant is to be
written in the heart (Jer. 31. 33).

Our Lord was well aware that this deeper piety would not
be easily won even by the Law-abiding Jew. A great decision
was to be made in all seriousness (Lk. 14. 26–33); the very
fact that such a decision was to be so gravely made shows
that our Lord contemplated not merely a greater impetus
for the externals of the Law but a searching change of heart

and outlook; once made, this decision must be relentlessly
executed (Lk. 14. 26). Nor was the decision proposed as a
matter of indifference—it was to be the necessary condition
of the eternal reward (Lk. 17. 33). Yet man's free-will
remained; the Father commanded man to hear His Son
(Mk. 9. 6) but man was not forced to hear. Christ allowed
the unbelievers to desert Him, and even to the Apostles He
said: Will you also go away? (Jn. 6. 68–69).

B. Jesus the Redeemer-Messias

The Fall of man had been followed by a divine promise of
spiritual recovery (Gen. 3. 15). This blessing was to come
through the family of Abraham (Gen. 12. 1–7) by way of the
branch represented by Jacob ("Israel"; Gen. 28. 10–15).
The promise was inherited by Jacob's son, Juda (Gen. 49.
8–12) and found its first, partial, fulfilment in David the
king, descended from Juda's tribe (2 Kg. 7. 16); David's
dynasty, despite misfortunes, was to reign for ever. In the
prophetic period this divinely guaranteed hope centred in
more marked fashion upon an individual king of David's line
(Ez. 34. 11 f.). While the prophets repeated that Yahweh
would descend in person to work the redemption of His
people (Is. 49. 26) they also insisted that a great leader would
come like a second David; like David, he would come from
Bethlehem (Mic. 5. 2). From the Davidic stock there would
spring a wise king to rule not Israel alone but the whole
world in a golden age (Is. 11. 1–16), one shepherd over
Israel like David the shepherd-king come back from the
dead (Ez. 34. 23 f.). The presence of this mysteriously born
king (Is. 7. 14) would be a guarantee that Yahweh had in
truth come to save His people. The prophet even dared to
call him "Mighty God, everlasting Father, peaceful Prince"
(Is. 9. 6) to whom would be converted a "remnant" of the
people of Israel (Is. 10. 21). Yet how was this "conversion"

to be wrought? Not without suffering and not for Israel alone, by one who was to die and so to expiate the sins of Israel and of the world (Is. 49. 1–12; 53. 1–12; Zach. 12.8—13.1).

This great prophetic canvas is a seeming daub of clashing colours in confusing shapes. It presents a figure half-man half-God, rejected in his own kingdom yet master of the world, peaceful warrior and conqueror vanquished, done to death and reigning for ever. If there is any harmony in the picture, it will need a God to show it.

i. *A Progressive Revelation*

Works are dangerous things if they mean one thing for the speaker and another for the hearer. In view, therefore, of the current Messianic hopes distorted by time it is not surprising if our Lord did not Himself use the word "Messias" but preferred the titles "Son of Man" and "Son of God".

The fact of this reserve is beyond doubt. Thus the demons were forbidden to make Him known as "the Holy One of God"—i.e. as the Messias, the great adversary of Satan (Mk. 1. 24–25). The Apostles received the same command even in the last year of His life (Mk. 8. 30). The reserve extended to many of our Lord's great miracles which were worked in private and often accompanied by an injunction to silence (cf. Mk. 7. 36; 8. 26; cf. also Mk. 1. 44; 5. 43). It extended also to certain of His doctrines (Mk. 4. 10–12).

The reason for this reserve had its political and its religious side. Time was needed for the instruction of the Apostles at least, but this time would not be granted if the excitable Galileans were to proclaim a Holy War with this Messias as their unwilling Captain—Rome would soon put an end to that! In the religious order, too, the doctrine was such and the audience was such that the new revelation must be allowed to soak in, it could not be driven in.

ii. *A Discriminating Revelation*

Different patients need different treatment, and our Lord's were of three kinds: His own chosen Apostles, the multitude, the religious leaders. The first group was thoughtful if slow of understanding (Mk. 8. 17–21), the second enthusiastic but fickle and shallow (Jn. 6. 15, 67), the third was hostile from the beginning (Mk. 2.1—3.6).

To the Apostles Jesus revealed Himself as the Messias in the first year of His ministry (Mk. 8. 29). At the end of the year they were completely convinced, though they did not yet realize to the full the spiritual nature of His mission, still less the suffering which that mission was to entail (Mk. 8. 33). In the second year, our Lord strove to make His Apostles familiar with the idea of His coming passion and death. It was necessary that they should know the truth more quickly than others since they were to be the missionary nucleus of the new Kingdom.

With the ordinary folk things were different. To them our Lord made an indirect appeal by the dignity of His person, by His doctrine, by His miracles. But in spite of precautions an atmosphere of political Messianism was produced; our Lord refused, therefore, to accept a recognition of Messiahship from the crowds until the last week of His public life (Mk. 11. 9–10).

Towards the Pharisees His attitude was one of sorrowful anger (Mk. 3. 5). It was impossible to instruct the unwilling; He could only state His claims and condemn their blindness (Jn. 9. 41).

Some privileged souls enjoyed a high degree of our Lord's confidence. Such were Nicodemus (Jn. 3. 1–15), the Samaritan woman (Jn. 4. 26), the man born blind (Jn. 9. 37). In these cases Jesus reserved His liberty to act outside the general plan of progressive revelation.

iii. *The Public Revelation: our Lord's Mission is Spiritual*

The Baptist's message had been a call not of the nation to arms but of the individual to repentance (Lk. 3. 3–8); it had prepared for One who promised the rule of the Spirit in the heart (Mk. 1. 8). The adversary therefore was not to be Rome but Satan who, seeking to divert the great Messianic attack on his kingdom, lurks behind all the false material views which on every page of the Gospel threaten to paralyse the spiritual message of Christ.

Satan's first attack was frontal and betrayed his technique, hence the history of the Temptations of our Lord is the key to the Gospel story. The representative of the powers of evil sought to persuade Christ successively to comfort, ostentation, worldly ambition (Lk. 4. 1–13), at the expense of suffering, meekness and a purely spiritual kingdom. Too weak for success in that quarter he concentrated his forces on the flanks where he proved more successful. Hence we find the material Messianic outlook not only amongst the ordinary folk (Jn. 6. 15) but amonst the disciples of the Baptist (Lk. 7. 19–20) and even, to some degree, in the leader of the Apostolic band (Mk. 8. 33).

With infinite patience our Lord sought by action as well as by word to guide the Jewish mind into more spiritual ways. He showed from the outset that His war was against Satan and his kingdom (Mk. 1. 23–28); He stormed and captured the diabolic fortress even within the soul (Mk. 2. 1–11). Indeed, so much was His warfare waged on Satanic territory that He was scornfully called "the friend of sinners" (Lk. 7. 34). It was in the spiritual sphere, too, that He exercised His authority (Mt. 5. 20, 22, 28) and He condemned not the arrogance of the Roman overlords but the pride of the spiritual leaders of the people (Mt. 23. 1–39).

It should have been clear that our Lord was no political agitator; He roundly affirmed that the material things which

were Cæsar's must be duly rendered (Mk. 12. 17), and even
the abused power of Pilate was recognized, for it was "from
above" (Jn. 19. 11). Nevertheless in this obvious spirituality
of our Lord's mission the crowds did not see an insuperable
obstacle to the possibility of His political Messiahship. The
Messias of their dreams was to secure a material kingdom,
it is true, but he would do so with a spiritual end in view—
the universal observance of the Law. The Law? The interpretation of Jesus (cf. Mt. c. 5) might lead to misgivings but
He had not abrogated the Law (Mt. 5. 17). The Kingdom?
His description of the new Kingdom by means of parable
(cf. Mt. c. 13) was too mysterious to be disturbing (Mt. 13. 11).

Meanwhile, our Lord's personal prestige was growing. At
Nain (Lk. 7. 16) He was saluted as a great prophet. Despite
His own injunctions (Mk. 5. 43) the resurrection of Jairus's
daughter made a stir throughout the province (Mt. 9. 26).
True, He did not conduct Himself as a would-be conqueror,
nor was His origin as mysterious as they would have expected
(the Nazarenes thought they knew it well enough! Mk. 6. 3),
but Messianism was in the air and a spark would ignite it.

It was at Bethsaida Julias in the spring-tide which opened
our Lord's second year of preaching. No small enthusiasm
had persuaded five thousand men to follow Him (Jn. 6. 2);
one more marvel would bring a crisis. Jesus did not hesitate.
For a whole year He had laboured by hint, suggestion and
implication to raise their hopes to a spiritual plane; it was
now time for open speech and for the action which would
demand it. The miraculous feeding of the five thousand
produced the crisis—an outburst of revolutionary enthusiasm from which Jesus was forced to take refuge. But
it was clear that He could not for long escape their misguided zeal (Jn. 6. 15), and so on the following day at
Capharnaum He spoke to them clearly of His entirely
spiritual Messianic programme (Jn. 6. 26–72). He made no
mention of the Law but asked for unquestioning faith in

His person. He spoke not of their earthly Messianic Kingdom but only of eternal life. He asked for disciples, not recruits. They were astonished, disappointed, unbelieving. The hostile elements pointed out that He could not have descended from Heaven, as He claimed, since they knew His parents. But there was no need for the argument, the material outlook had already done its work. The Galilean ministry had failed and Jesus found Himself abandoned by all but the Twelve.

Rejected in Galilee, our Lord turned to Jerusalem. There too He maintained a cautious reserve with regard to the dangerous title of "Messias"; He preferred to insist on the spiritual character of His work (Jn. 5. 21–30). His doctrine did not meet with favour (Jn. 5. 18, 38–47) and He retired to Galilee (Jn. 7. 1). A few months later He refused to join the pilgrimage to Jerusalem for the feast of Tabernacles lest it should prove the occasion of a Messianic demonstration by the Galileans and by the lower orders in Jerusalem (Jn. 7. 2–13). Instead, He went up to Jerusalem as a private person (Jn. 7. 10) and, once there, presented Himself as the source of spiritual life (Jn. 7. 37–39) and as the shepherd who would keep that life in the flock even at the price of His own death (Jn. 10. 1–21). In return He asked, as in Galilee, for a complete surrender of mind and heart (Jn. 8. 31). Despite our Lord's reserve, however, the term "Messias" passed conjecturally from lip to lip in Jerusalem (Jn. 7. 40–43). At the feast of Dedication the plain question was put to Him: if thou be the Christ, tell us plainly (Jn. 10. 22–30). Even had the question been put in a friendly spirit He would not have answered directly; He could not answer briefly without deceiving them since He was not their imagined Messias—He was very much more.

The silence was to be broken before His death. If Israel was to refuse Him, it was to have no excuse; now it must take its opportunity or know its crime. Nearly four months after the feast of Dedication our Lord publicly accepted the

clearly Messianic title "Son of David" from the blind man
near Jericho (Lk. 18. 38), and on the Sunday before His
death He entered the Holy City as Messias, not with armed
force but "meek and sitting upon an ass" (Mt. 21. 5). On
the Thursday He stood before the grand Senate of Israel, a
self-confessed Messias whose kingdom was not of this world
and whose glory was in the clouds of heaven (Mk. 14. 61–62;
cf. Jn. 18. 36).

iv. *The Public Revelation: Hints of the Passion*

Jesus reserved to His intimate circle the clear prophecies
of His passion and death. The fuller revelation would have
proved a scandal for others and He contented Himself with
the darker hints which would be understood only in the
light of future events. Thus at the opening of the Galilean
ministry He speaks in allegory of the days when "the bride-
groom will be taken away" (Mk. 2. 19–20), and at the close
of that ministry, of His flesh "given for the life of the world"
(Jn. 6. 52). Six months later, in Jerusalem, He describes
Himself publicly as the Good Shepherd who lays down his
life for his sheep (Jn. 10. 15–18). These and other sugges-
tions (e.g. Jn. 12. 20–25), pointed as they are, contrast
sharply with the clear predictions made to the circle of
Apostles.

v. *Revelation to the Apostles; the Redemptive Death*

In His second year of ministry our Lord devoted Himself
more particularly to the formation of His Apostles. Like
the crowds, they had seen His miracles and heard His word.
Unlike the crowds, they had kept His constant company
(Lk. 22. 28), received His plainer teaching of the mysteries
of the Kingdom (Mk. 4. 11), shared in His miraculous
powers (Mk. 6. 13) and learned from day to day ever more
of His message as they preached it to others (Mk. 6. 7–12).

Yet the Apostles were painfully slow of understanding

(Mk. 8. 17–21). It is true that many of them had recognized the Messiahship of Jesus from the beginning (Jn. 1. 41, 45, 49), and that this recognition grew in the space of a year into the deepest appreciation of His personal dignity (Mt. 14. 33). Yet their misunderstanding of His exclusively spiritual mission was profound and persistent (Lk. 24. 21). As for His passion, the very idea so contradicted their undisturbed convictions that they could remain almost incredibly deaf to the plainest speech; on three such occasions the evangelists remark the fact (Mk. 8. 32 f.; 9. 31; Lk. 18. 34).

(a) THREE PREDICTIONS OF THE PASSION

Though the understanding of the Apostles was yet to be persuaded, their hearts were already won. The time had not been wasted; whatever happened, they were His. Our Lord received this assurance at the end of His first year of ministry (Jn. 6. 69). Moreover, they were at last coming to know Him for what He was and a few months later at Cæsarea Philippi, the awaited declaration came. While many, misled by our Lord's demeanour or rather by their mistaken hopes in His regard, were thinking vaguely of Elias or Jeremias come to announce the Messias, Peter at least answered without hesitation that his Master was the Messias (Mk. 8. 29)—more, He was the Son of the Living God (Mt. 16. 14–16). The Apostles realized at that moment that our Lord was a Messias far greater than they had once expected. This realization achieved, Jesus knew that the time had come to announce His passion and death. He knew that now their loyal conviction could sustain the shock even if their understanding recoiled before it (Mk. 8. 32 f.). Cæsarea Philippi was therefore the turning-point of Christ's revelation to the Apostles.

He sounded the note of coming death immediately and it is heard in the very promise of the primacy to Peter. Like one about to depart from the earth He bequeathed to Peter the vice-regency of His Kingdom (Mt. 16. 18–19). There followed the first clear prediction of the Passion (Mk. 8. 31–33). It shocked Peter; death for him spelt failure, and the promise of subsequent resurrection must have been buried under the weight of his alarm. He expostulated, but his Master rebuked him and went on relentlessly to promise a similar fate for His faithful disciples (Mk. 8. 34–38).

A week of sorrowful reflection followed. Perhaps the shocking words were not to be taken too literally. After all, the Master had spoken in metaphors before and had rebuked them for not realizing it (Mk. 8. 14–21). He had called death by the name of sleep (Mk. 5. 39), perhaps there was something of the sort here?

When the week had passed (Mk. 9. 1–12), Peter with James and John was permitted to see the reverse side of this gloomy picture of suffering and death. The glory of the Transfiguration had been already hinted in our Lord's prophecy of resurrection and in His acceptance of Peter's act of faith in the Son of the Living God. But if the Transfiguration was an encouragement to that faith, it was a warning, too, and a necessary one. The presence of Moses and Elias invited them to reflect that, however unexpected may be the words of Jesus, they were loyally supported by the Law and the Prophets, and however strange His predictions the voice of the Father bade them believe: Hear ye Him! But the glory of the whole scene carried Peter away, effacing the memory of the prophecy. He had seen the Messias in His glory, he had seen the precursor Elias who had surely come to announce the Kingdom and to anoint the King. He therefore proposed a temporary dwelling until the hour of manifestation should strike. But Elias disappeared, the glory faded and once again the note of warning came: the glorious truth was not to be published, there was to be no rallying of supporters to this Messias who had only for a moment revealed His glory.

The second prediction of the Passion was made a few weeks later and the Apostles still "understood not the word" (Mk. 9. 29–31). They were far indeed from understanding when they disputed for dignities in the material kingdom to come!

The third prophecy (cf. Mk. 10. 32–45) was made on the way to Jerusalem when the fatal Pasch was approaching and when the final resolve on our Lord's death had already been taken (Jn. 11. 45–53). This third prediction is more detailed: the Romans enter into the picture, the mocking, scourging and insult; moreover, all was a fulfilment of ancient prophecy (Lk. 18. 31). And yet, such is the power of ingrained opinion, "they understood not the things that were said". Again the evangelists note the earthly ambition of the Apostles which Jesus patiently corrects. In doing so, our Lord explains in a word the purpose of His death—it is to be a ransom for many; the Master was to sell His life as a faithful slave would sell it for his owner (Mk. 10. 45).

(b) THE LAST SUPPER

But the hint of "ransom" was not enough for the Apostles and the question must have remained in their minds: what is the purpose of the death which He seems to court so deliberately (Jn. 11. 8, 16)? What connexion could it possibly have with the new Kingdom and with the Eternal Life that He has promised? At the Last Supper the questions were answered and the Apostles believed, though full understanding would only come to them later.

When God had concluded the ancient Covenant with Israel, Moses the mediator had taken the blood of the sacrifice and had said: This is the blood of the Covenant (Ex. 24. 8). The sacrifice had been the human signature giving effect to the Treaty—the Alliance was signed in blood. On this night, fifteen hundred years later, Jesus having taken the chalice said: This is my blood of the new Covenant (Mk. 14. 22–24). The echo of the words of Moses was unmistakable, but the victim of the sacrifice was now Christ Himself. The prophets had promised a new Covenant (Jer. 31. 31–34) and at the Last Supper this Covenant was ratified, Christ Himself being at once its mediator and its sacrifice. He was not to die until the morrow, but at the Last Supper by solemn priestly act He freely offered that death and became from then and for ever the victim of Calvary. Aptly figuring His death by separate consecration, He made His body and blood really present, symbolically and not yet actually divided. It was mysteriously the same body which was to hang on the cross, the same blood which was to be shed on Calvary. His words so joined the Supper with the Passion as to make it clear that His death was a sacrifice freely offered to the Father for the remission of sins. Thus He explained, as fully as the mystery would permit, the religious significance of the death He had so openly announced to His Apostles.

There remained one question still: what of the Great Promise of Capharnaum (Jn. 6. 48–59)? Belief in the Bread of Life had been made a test-case of loyalty; on that issue, which therefore must have belonged to the very centre of His mission, Jesus had been prepared to see His year's work in Galilee vanish (Jn. 6. 67 f.). The promise received its fulfilment and explanation at the Last Supper: Take ye and eat! Here also the Old Testament would serve to explain the New. Under the Mosaic Law the blood of the sacrificial peace-offering was offered to God but the flesh was eaten by priest and people (Lev. 7. 11–16). Here in this new peace offering ("making peace", as St Paul was to say in his epistle to the Colossians 1. 20, "through the blood of His cross") the Mediator and the Victim was also the Food.

The Supper draws thus into unity the three apparently unrelated notions of the new Kingdom (established by a new

Covenant), the suffering Messias, the Bread of Life. For this reason it is the almost indispensable key to the Messianic plan. It so declares the essence of the mission of Jesus and so communicates its effects that it becomes the central liturgical act of the Kingdom which Christ founded: Do this in commemoration of Me! (Lk. 22. 19; cf. 1 Cor. 10. 16; 11. 17–34).

(c) THE RESURRECTION

The light of Christ's risen body was the revelation which surpassed and explained all others and resolved for the Apostles the dark riddle of His death. It was the visible proof that Satan, by whom death had come into the world, had been finally conquered (1 Cor. 15. 20–22). Death, and much more, had been swallowed up in victory; the head of the serpent had been crushed according to the old promise (Gen. 3. 15). The Resurrection made new men of the Apostles, it changed them from sorrowing mourners into confident missionaries (cf. Lk. 24. 21 with Ac. 2. 24–32). It gave them the conviction which, armed with the gift of the Spirit, sent them forth to preach the good news to every creature.

C. JESUS THE MESSIAS, SON OF GOD

We have seen with what force the inspired Hebrew literature presented the dignity of the future Messias-king. His place was in honour at God's right hand (Ps. 109. 1), his existence stretched back to the distant past (Mic. 5. 2) and forward as long as the sun and moon should endure (Ps. 71. 5), he was the very Son of God (Ps. 2. 7) begotten "before the daystar" (Ps. 109. 3, Septuagint translation). He was to rule with the very power and majesty of Yahweh (Mic. 5. 3 f.); the names which express his person and mission are "God-with-us" (Is. 7. 14), "Yahweh-our-justice" (Jer. 23.

6); he is even said to be in his own person "God the mighty" (Is. 9. 6). To these astounding expressions the later uninspired Jewish literature did less than justice, yet even here (especially in the "apocalyptic literature") we are left with the impression that the Messias is to be little less than Yahweh Himself. But the final conclusion was never reached: Jewish interpretation did not identify the Messias with Yahweh the only God. For this reason our Lord could not say outright: I am your God. For a Jew this would mean either the attempted dethronement of Yahweh or the assertion of two Gods. With His customary prudence our Lord approached the delicate business of the revelation of His divinity.

i. *Implicit Revelations*

With unequalled authority Jesus taught in the synagogues (Mk. 1. 22). No prophet, not even the Messias, could forgive sins—yet He forgave them (Mk. 2. 1–12). He claimed to be master of the Sabbath, most immutable of divine institutions (Mk. 2. 28). Again and again He dared to use the bold formula: "It was said to them of old (by God) . . . But I say to you . . ." (Mt. 5. 17–48), speaking as one who would venture on His own authority to reform the sacred Law.

In person He claimed to be greater than Solomon (Lk. 11. 31), greater even than David (Mk. 12. 37), greater than the prophets after whom He was sent as the crowning gift of the Lord of the vineyard of Israel (Mk. 12. 1–9). Even the angels were His servants and ministers (Mk. 1. 13; Mt. 13. 41). Most surprising of all, He made Himself the very focus of religious devotion and not merely its model, claiming for Himself the personal love and devotion that the prophets had claimed for Yahweh (Mt. 10. 37). The sinner was forgiven because she loved Him well, forgiven with the dignified condescension of placated Majesty itself (Lk. 7. 36–50).

ii. *Explicit Revelations*

(a) TO THE APOSTLES

The Apostles were convinced of the superhuman dignity of Jesus sooner than they were of the necessity of His suffering. After little more than a year of His company, Peter had proclaimed Him Son of the Living God (Mt. 16. 16). His words were almost an echo of the impulsive exclamation of the Apostles some eight months earlier (Mt. 14. 33), but this time the declaration was made so deliberately and, as is evident from Christ's reply, with such a depth of meaning that only the Father could have revealed it. Indeed the Father Himself confirmed the title for the benefit of the chosen three, one week later on the mount of Transfiguration (Mk. 9. 6).

To a wider circle of disciples some weeks afterwards (Lk. 10. 17–22) our Lord revealed the secret of His relationship with the Father. He told them that the nature of the Father was such that only He, the Son, could know and reveal Him and that the nature of the Son was such that only the Father could know Him. This sentence places the Son on the Father's level which is far above the unaided capacity of creature minds.

The mystery contained in those words was put to the Apostles even more plainly in our Lord's last long discourse to them on the night of the Supper: Do you not believe that I am in the Father and the Father in Me? (Jn. 14. 10). Only the light of glory could take the human mind further than this, but St Thomas summed it up in his tardy confession: My Lord and my God!

(b) PUBLIC TEACHING IN JERUSALEM

The declared purpose of the Fourth Gospel was to state and to demonstrate the divinity of Jesus (Jn. 20. 31). It is

St John, therefore, who reports at some length the discourses in Jerusalem addressed to an audience prepared in mind, if not in heart, for a deeper theological statement. After the Galilean rejection our Lord gave Jerusalem its opportunity. His audience understood Him well enough: if He called God His Father, He intended to make Himself equal to God (Jn. 5. 17–18). Four months later at the feast of Tabernacles (Jn. 8. 58 f.) He asserted His timeless existence: Before Abraham was made, *I am*. Again their judgment was unerring—only Yahweh had spoken thus (Ex. 3. 14)—and they took up stones to punish the blasphemy (cf. Lev. 24. 16). In December (Jn. 10. 30–33) His words were even clearer: The Father and I are One Thing. The Jews were provoked to a further attempt upon His life because, as they said, being a man He made Himself God. They did not guess that He might be man and God.

(c) THE FINAL TESTIMONY

Jesus was condemned to death for blasphemy. Claim to be the Messias might be madness but it did not constitute a capital charge; blasphemy did (Deut. 13. 2–11). The two questions: "Christ?", "Son of God?", clearly distinguished in St Luke's Gospel (Lk. 22. 66–71) were distinct also in the mind of Caiaphas. A Messias claiming to sit "at the right hand of God" was, in Caiaphas's opinion, claiming more than Messiahship. Caiaphas therefore proceeds: Art thou then the Son of God? Now, if ever, solemnly adjured by the high tribunal of Israel, now, if ever, had there been any misunderstanding, Jesus was bound to retract or explain His claim. He did neither. He died maintaining it.

ADDITIONAL NOTE: THE GOSPEL SEQUENCE

The following brief list gives the sequence adopted as a basis in the foregoing chapter; it will serve to place in their approximate period the incidents there referred to. Of the various probable theories it is a matter of practical necessity to choose one, we have therefore adopted the theory of a two-year Ministry, and the dates (A.D. 28–30) often assigned to it, as a working hypothesis. With the same reserve the suggested inversion of chapters 5 and 6 of St John's Gospel has been accepted. This same Gospel provides the information (in terms of the Jewish liturgical year) which alone makes possible a dated account of our Lord's life. Of the feasts which John mentions, the Pasch occurred in March-April, the feast of Tabernacles in September-October, the feast of Dedication in December. The feast of Pentecost which he does not mention by name occurred in May-June. We have identified his references thus: the Pasch of Jn. 2. 13 is the first Pasch (in March, A.D. 28); the Pasch of Jn. 6. 4 is the second Pasch (in April, A.D. 29); the unnamed "feast" of Jn. 5. 1 is the feast of Pentecost (in June, A.D. 29); the feast of Tabernacles of Jn. 7. 2 is "Tabernacles" of A.D. 29 (occurring, that year, in October); the Dedication feast of Jn. 10. 22 is the December of the same year. The Pasch of Jn. 12. 1 is, of course, the last Pasch and, according to the "two-year" hypothesis, the third (in April of A.D. 30).

References: For sections found in more than one Gospel reference is usually made to Mark; we except the "Peræan Ministry" period (the great "central section" of Luke: 9.51—18.14) of which Matthew and Mark say little, here reference is made to Luke and John. An asterisk marks a passage which belongs, in the main, only to the evangelist quoted.

I. BIRTH AND HIDDEN LIFE

*Jn. 1. 1–18; *Lk. 1. 5–80; *Mt. 1. 18–25; *Lk. 2. 1–38; *Mt. 2. 1–22; *Lk. 2. 39–52.

II. PUBLIC MINISTRY

(1) PRELUDE: JUDEA-GALILEE-JUDEA. OCTOBER, A.D. 27 TO MAY, A.D. 28.

Mk. 1. 1–11; Lk. 3. 23–38 (and cf. Mt. 1. 1–17); Lk. 4. 1–13 (January-February, A.D. 28); *Jn. 1.19—3.36 (March, A.D. 28, First Pasch); Mk. 6. 17–20 (May).

(2) GALILEAN MINISTRY. MAY, A.D. 28 TO OCTOBER, A.D. 29.

i. *Early Activity. May*, A.D. 28

Mk. 1. 14; *Jn. 4. 4–54; *Lk. 4. 16–22; Mk. 1. 21–39; Mk. 1. 16–20; Mk. 1. 40–45.

ii. *Pharisaic Opposition. May to June*, A.D. 28

Mk. 2.1—3.6.

iii. *Inauguration of the New Society. June*, A.D. 28

Mk. 3. 13–19; Mt. 5.1—7.29; Mk. 4. 1–34 (but cf. section (2) iv.).

iv. *Great Miracles, Galilean Anticlimax. June*, A.D. 28 *to April*, A.D. 29

Lk. 7. 1–10; *Lk. 7. 11–16; Lk. 7. 17–35; Mk. 4. 1–34 (in the order of time; in the order of ideas it belongs to section (2) iii); Mk. 4. 35–41 (December?); Mk. 5.1—6.56 (and cf. *Mt. 9. 26; *Mt. 14. 28–33); *Jn. 6. 14, 15, 22–72 (April, A.D. 29, Second Pasch).

v. *Jerusalem, Galilee Again. June*, A.D. 29

*Jn. 5. 1–47 (Pentecost); *Jn. 7. 1; Mk. 7. 1–23.

vi. *Phœnicia, Decapolis, Galilee.*
June to October, A.D. 29

Mk. 7.24—8.21; Mk. 8. 22–26; Mk. 8. 27–30 (and cf. Mt. 16. 12–23); Mk. 8.31—9.49 (and cf. Mt. 18. 1–35).

(3) Peræan Ministry (Journeys to Jerusalem).
October, A.D. 29 to April, A.D. 30.

i. *First Journey (for "Tabernacles") and After.*
October to December, A.D. 29

*Jn. 7. 2–13; *Lk. 9. 51–56; *Jn. 7.14—10.21; *Lk. 9.57—10.42; Lk. 11. 1–54 (and cf. *Mt. 9. 27–34); Lk. 12.1—13.21.

ii. *Second Journey (for "Dedication").*
December, A.D. 29 *to February,* A.D. 30

*Lk. 13. 22; *Jn. 10. 22–42; Lk. 13.23—17.10.

iii. *Third Journey. February to April,* A.D. 30

*Lk. 17. 11; Lk. 17. 12–18. 20; *Jn. 11. 1–56 (March, A.D. 30); Lk. 18. 31–34; Mk. 10. 35–45; Lk. 18.35—19.28; Mk. 14. 3–9.

III. PASSION. RESURRECTION. ASCENSION.

April–May, A.D. 30

(1) Passion and Death. April, A.D. 30

Mk. 11. 1–11 (Palm Sunday; cf. *Mt. 21. 4–5; *Lk. 19. 41–44; *Jn. 12. 20–36); Mk. 11. 12–19 (Monday); Mk. 11.20—13.32 (Tuesday; cf. *Mt. 23. 8–36); Mk. 14. 10–11 (Wednesday); Mk. 14. 12–72 (Thursday; cf. *Lk. 22. 27–30; *Jn. 13.31—17.26); Mk. 15. 1–47 (Friday; cf. *Jn. 18. 34–38; *Lk. 23. 4–17; *Jn. 19. 9–11); *Mt. 27. 62–66 (Saturday).

(2) Resurrection and After. April–May, a.d. 30

Mk. 16. 1–13 (Easter Sunday; cf. *Mt. 28. 11–15; *Lk. 24. 13–35); *Jn. 20. 24–29 (Jerusalem, one week later); *Jn. 21. 1–23 (Galilee, later); Mk. 16. 15–18 (Galilee, later); *Lk. 24. 44–49 (Jerusalem, in May); Mk. 16. 19–20 (Mt Olivet, May).

CHAPTER XII

THE NEW KINGDOM

"The Kingdom of God" was a phrase constantly on our Lord's lips; it was the message of His earliest preaching (Mt. 4. 17) and the theme of His doctrine in all the towns of Galilee (Mt. 9. 35); its announcement was the very purpose of His coming (Lk. 4. 42–43). It was this Kingdom that the Twelve were sent to preach (Mt. 10. 7) and the Seventy-two disciples (Lk. 10. 9). It constituted the principal subject of our Lord's teaching in the forty days that followed His Resurrection (Ac. 1. 3).

Neither the expression itself nor its basic meaning was new to Christ's fellow countrymen. The inspired writers had taught them that Yahweh was King of all things because He had made all things (Ps. 23. 1–10). In addition to this fundamental right to universal kingship, Yahweh had a special royal claim on Israel whom He had delivered from Egypt and made into an independent nation (Ps. 113. 1–2). He had made His royal will known to this chosen people through the Mosaic legislation, and in proportion as this legislation was observed so did Israel become God's kingdom in fact as it was always His kingdom by right.

The purpose of this deliverance which Yahweh the King had effected was the formation of a nation free to serve Him (Ex. 15. 13–18)—it was a political salvation with a religious end, namely the acknowledgment of the kingship of Yahweh. The resultant "Kingdom of God" was therefore a suitable foreshadowing of the more sublime salvation to be wrought by our Lord (1 Cor. 10. 1–11). Hence it is not surprising that Jesus should choose a term which was so traditional, so fundamentally exact and so capable of immense development and clarification. In its ultimate essence the Kingdom will always remain the same, for it is the practical recognition of the Will of God (Mt. 6. 10), but that divine Will can receive and does receive a new manifestation through the unrivalled revelation of the only Son (Jn. 1. 18). This new manifestation would probably make, and actually does make (Mt. 5. 17–48), greater demands on those who benefit by it. The experience of divine generosity in the past would lead Israel to expect a greater divine help in proportion to the greater demands; the expectation was not frustrated but surpassed beyond measure (Eph. 1. 3–8).

What are the characteristics of the Kingdom as announced by our Lord, the Kingdom which is said to be "at hand" when He begins His public ministry (Mt. 4. 17)? Is the Kingdom to be established on earth or in heaven? Is it to be predominantly Jewish? Is the Messias to govern it in person? What are its enemies? What are its weapons? What are the privileges of its citizens? What is its ultimate goal?

I. THE "KINGDOM OF GOD": A COMPLEX NOTION

Traditional Jewish opinion had distinguished two periods in the future history of mankind: an earthly stage ("the days of the Messias") and a heavenly one. To the first, it gave the title of "the Kingdom of God", the second was called "the World to come". By drawing the two ideas together in the single phrase "the Kingdom of God", our Lord demonstrated implicitly the unity of the divine plan for the here and the hereafter and showed that the fruits of His Messianic work would be manifested fully and finally only in the world to come. But in addition to these two different, though not independent, notions, the term "Kingdom of God" is capable of a third meaning which might be better rendered "the Rule of God". This means the actual reign of God in those human souls which show by their lives that they recognize God's royal rights. It is only of such souls that the Kingdom of God in heaven is composed, for it is "the just" who "shall shine in the Kingdom of their Father" (Mt. 13. 43). But it will be seen that this is not the case in Christ's Kingdom of God on earth, as it was not the case in the old Israelitic Kingdom of God.

The notion, therefore, suggested by our Lord's use of the phrase is complex and not simple, and Jesus hinted as much when He referred to its mysterious nature (Mt. 13. 11). The precise meaning which our Lord intends to give to the phrase will have to be determined in each case by the context. Thus, for instance, when He applies to the Kingdom the conventional Jewish pictures of "the World to come" (e.g. the banquet image as opposed to the exterior darkness, Mt. 8. 11–12) it is clear that He is speaking of the Kingdom in heaven. On the other hand, when the Kingdom is said to contain bad elements as well as good (Mt. 13. 47–50) it is evident that the Kingdom is being considered according to its aspect of an external society on earth which includes imperfect members. This last is again plainly different from the third possible meaning of God's rule in the obedient soul, a meaning which is found, for instance, in the "Our Father" (Mt. 6. 10). In this text, the petition: "Thy Kingdom come!" is equivalent to: "Thy will be done", and our Lord is teaching the Apostles to pray for the recognition of God's will by human souls. It will be noticed that, taken in this sense of "the rule of God", the Kingdom is said to "come"—to enter into man. It must be understood in one, or both, of its two other possible senses when man is said to enter the Kingdom (e.g. Jn. 3. 5). It is clear, too, that this "coming" of the Kingdom is likely to be a slow process; there may, however, be a period or periods of history providentially disposed to enable this "rule" to make spectacular advances; in this way, the destruction of Jerusalem (in A.D. 70), marking as it did the end of the old epoch, could be said to constitute a special "coming" of the Kingdom (Lk. 21. 31).

Naturally, these three notions are not entirely independent. Internal recognition of the divine will is required and secured by loyal membership of Christ's society on earth, and this loyalty in turn will guarantee membership of the eternal Kingdom of God in heaven. Although, therefore, the central subject of the discussion which follows is the Kingdom under the aspect of an external society on earth, the other two aspects are not positively excluded.

II. THE KINGDOM OF GOD: A SOCIETY ON EARTH

Our Lord made it clear that the Kingdom of God is not merely a mansion in the world to come but rather a tower which has its foundations in the earth though its head is in the clouds of heaven.

The parables dealing with the nature of the Kingdom (Mt. 13. 1–35) bring out its earthly aspect. Thus in the parable of the wheat and cockle, the "field" in which each is sown is "the world" (Mt. 13. 38). In the period which elapses between sowing-time and final harvest (the end of the world, Mt. 13. 39), the work of the Son of Man is countered by the activity of the devil. The circumstances, therefore, are those of an earthly Kingdom and not of an exclusively heavenly one.[1] Similar to the parable of the wheat and the cockle is the parable of the fishing-net (Mt. 13. 47–50) which contains bad fish as well as good; the final selection is not made until the end of the world. The same conclusion is indicated by the images of the leaven (Mt. 13. 33) and of the seed (Mk. 4. 26–29) very slowly making their power felt. Such images are quite incompatible with the

[1] With a view to the interpretation of other texts (e.g. Mt. 16. 28) it is important to notice that this period of the Kingdom on earth is referred to as the Kingdom of the Son (Mt. 13. 41) as opposed to the Kingdom of the Father in heaven (Mt. 13. 43).

sudden divine intervention (Mt. 24. 30) which means the
end of all earthly things and the beginning of the Kingdom
in heaven.[1]

Outside the parables the same characteristic of the Kingdom appears. Like the age of the Law and the Prophets,
extending from Moses to the Baptist (Mt. 11. 12–13) it
constitutes a period of human history on earth. Indeed, the
Kingdom is already inaugurated by Christ in person; this
is evident from the success of His direct attack upon the
opposing kingdom which is that of Satan (Mt. 12. 22–29).
Moreover, the Kingdom is to continue on earth after our
Lord's departure, for He commits its keys to Peter (Mt. 16.
19; cf. 16. 21); it is because the sheep must be fed after He
has laid down His life for them that He appoints a shepherd
to look after them (Jn. 10. 15; cf. 21. 15–17).

How long will this earthly Kingdom endure? This was to
remain a divine secret (Mt. 24. 36), no doubt to keep before
humanity a salutary uncertainty of the duration of all its
works. Yet the period, it seems, would be long. The Gospel
must first be preached to all nations (Mt. 24. 14) and the
Kingdom must have time to grow to great size from very
small beginnings (Mt. 13. 31–33). It is not likened to a tent
which may be quickly folded and removed, it is like a house
built stoutly upon a rock to stand the storms of centuries
(Mt. 16. 18; cf. 7. 24–27). The Messias will be with His
Kingdom until the end of the world (Mt. 28. 20), invisibly
but powerfully present (Jn. 16. 7–15), but the duration of
these "days of the Messias", so disputed among the rabbis,
still remains a secret which it is not necessary to know
(2 Pet. 3. 1–18).

---

[1] St Matthew, who speaks most frequently of the Kingdom, very
often uses the term "Kingdom of the heavens". This phrase means
precisely the same thing as "Kingdom of God", but with Jewish delicacy
avoids the use of the Sacred Name. It therefore bears the same wide
meaning as we have indicated for the "Kingdom of God" and need not
be taken to refer exclusively to the Kingdom *in* heaven.

III. The Kingdom of God throughout the Earth

Our Lord's personal mission was addressed to Israel (Mt. 15. 24) and to Israel He first sent the Twelve (Mt. 10. 5). This course of action was dictated by divine fidelity to the promises made to Israel; even St Paul, ardent apostle of the Gentiles though he was, recognized this Jewish privilege (Ac. 13. 46).

Yet Jesus had other sheep not of the fold of Israel (Jn. 10. 16) and as Israel's rejection of Him became increasingly evident, He foretold in turn His own rejection of Israel as a nation and the entry of all people to the Kingdom (Mt. 8. 10–12). Nevertheless it was with real sorrow that He announced the destruction of Jerusalem (Mt. 23. 37–39), once the city of the Great King (Mt. 5. 35). It will be the capital of God's Kingdom no longer because the Kingdom is to be given to no single nation but to all those who will "bring forth the fruits thereof" (Mt. 21. 43). Thus Israel, first in the divine plan to receive the salvation of God, gave place to the Gentiles and "the last became first" (Lk. 13. 30).

After His Resurrection our Lord sends the Apostles to teach all nations (Mt. 28. 19). In this He fulfils the ancient promises which foreshadowed blessing through Abraham to all the earth (Gen. 12. 3), realizes Isaias' vision of world-obedience to Yahweh (Is. 2. 2–3), rules the kingdom of Daniel which triumphantly fills the whole earth (Dan. 2. 34, 35, 44).

Was the divine plan for Israel entirely frustrated then? St Paul answers "No!" As God had promised, the Messias Himself had come from the bosom of Israel (Rom. 9. 5) and some at least of Israel had embraced the gospel of Jesus (Rom. 11. 5), thus justifying the old prophecy which promised salvation to a "remnant" of Israel (e.g. Is. 7. 3; 10. 22). The time would even come when Israel as a nation, led by the example of the Gentiles (how strange a reversal of rôles!) would enter the Kingdom of Christ (Rom. 11. 11, 25–27).

IV. THE CONSTITUTIONAL AUTHORITY IN THE KINGDOM

What was to become of this Kingdom, destined to be world-wide, on the death of its Founder? Even human prudence would have insisted on a wise provision for the future. It is true that our Lord had promised His presence to the end (Mt. 28. 20), but it was not to be a visible presence (Mt. 26. 11), and yet some human authority was clearly required to guarantee the faithful transmission of Christ's teaching, to enroll men by the visible rite of Baptism, prudently to ensure that the cockle did not suffocate the wheat.

Faced with the opposition of the Pharisees and with the blindness of the crowds, our Lord devoted Himself to the particular instruction of twelve men to whom He confided the mysteries of the Kingdom (Mt. 13. 11). These were specially chosen to reap the fruit of Christ's work (Jn. 15. 16); He could only sow (Mt. 13. 37), they were to gather in the great harvest (Jn. 4. 38). It was to the Twelve, therefore, that He committed the office of teaching and of admission to the Kingdom (Mt. 28. 18–19). Upon them He conferred the power to perform the great Rite (Lk. 22. 19) which appears twenty years later as the very central liturgical act in the Kingdom (1 Cor. 11. 24 f.). They were to enjoy the widest jurisdiction in that Kingdom (Mt. 18. 15–18) which was to include a supreme judicial function in regard to its citizens (Jn. 20. 21).

At the head of all the lists of the Apostles (Mt. 10. 2; Mk. 3. 16; Lk. 6. 14; Ac. 1. 13) stands Simon Peter. It was for him to impart to the Apostles the unshakable faith which Christ's never-failing prayer (Jn. 11. 42) had asked on his behalf (Lk. 22. 31–32). Peter has the keys of the Kingdom on earth, the keys which fit the gate of heaven also (Mt. 16. 19); they are delivered to him by the One to whom they

rightly belong (Apoc. 3. 7). In the absence of the Good
Shepherd who died for His sheep (Jn. 10. 15) Peter is to
pasture them (Jn. 21. 15–17). Peter in his turn will die
(Jn. 21. 18–19) but the Kingdom must go on (Mt. 16. 18).
There is no doubt that our Lord made provision for the
more distant future of His Kingdom lest the gates of hell
should prevail and the rock-foundation crumble.

V. The Enemy of the Kingdom

The foes of the king are the foes of his kingdom, and it is
Satan who appears as the great adversary of our Lord—a
cunningly disguised adversary at first (Lk. 4. 1–13) but later
a baffled and openly vindictive enemy (Jn. 13. 2). Satan, too,
has his kingdom, firmly established before the coming of
Christ (Mt. 12. 28); it is so established and so universal that
he can confidently offer to make Jesus vice-regent of all the
kingdoms of the earth (Lk. 4. 5–7). This kingdom of evil,
bitterly opposed to the Kingdom of God, is nevertheless
essentially weaker. Thus our Lord, victor of the struggle in
the desert, shows by His effortless exorcism (Mt. 12. 22–29)
that the Kingdom of God has come. His effective commission
of the same powers to the seventy-two disciples is a certain
proof that Satan is falling from his high place (Lk. 10. 18),
The fortress of Satan, ceaselessly active against the Kingdom.
will yet be finally powerless (Mt. 16. 18).

Whence did Satan derive his kingdom? The narrative of
Genesis[1] shows that it was Satan who engineered the Fall
of man. The Sciptures had taught, and the contemporaries
of our Lord knew, that Adam's disobedience had earned
physical death and moral weakness for his descendants
(Ecclus. 25. 33; Wis. 2. 23–25). It is St Paul, however, who
gives the doctrine a clearer and fuller definition: "through
one man sin came into the world, and through sin death,

[1] Gen. c. 3.

and thus death spread to all men, because all had sinned"
(Rom. 5. 12, Westm. Version). As a consequence, there is in
every man a struggle with the passions, a struggle made
necessary by Adam's sin (Rom. 7. 7–25). This state of
rebellion, all too often successful, is the "reign of sin" which
is the same thing as the reign of Satan (cf. Rom. 7. 23;
Eph. 2. 1 f.; 2 Cor. 4. 4).

The enemy is by no means invincible (Rom. 6. 11–12),
but he is intangible and cannot be fought with material
weapons. The necessary armament is described by St Paul:
"Take ye up the full armour of God . . . your loins girt in
truth, and having on the breastplate of justness . . . taking
up withal the shield of faith wherewith ye shall be able to
quench all the fiery darts of the evil one" (Eph. 6. 13–16,
Westm. Version).

VI. The Armour of God

i. *Faith*

The absolute necessity of Faith is plainly taught in the
Gospels. Of all the inner dispositions required from the
citizens of the Kingdom (Mt. 5. 2–12) it is the most fundamental: "He that believeth not shall be condemned"
(Mk. 16. 16), and indeed "he that doth not believe (in the
only-begotten Son of God) is already judged" (Jn. 3. 18).
Unbelief bars the entrance to the Kingdom, but the simple
faith of the sinners who heard the Precursor opened a door
to them which was shut to the instructed Pharisaic elite
(Mt. 21. 31–32); for the Kingdom of God must be received
with the simplicity of a child (Mk. 10. 15). This is but
another aspect of the universality of the Kingdom; we might
call it "vertical" universality. We have already seen that the
Kingdom ignores national barriers and spreads horizontally
over the earth; we now see that it ignores intellectual
barriers also and penetrates downwards into the very

simplest classes of society. It can afford to do so because "the foolish things of this world" are made wise with the divine wisdom of Christ (1 Cor. 1. 17–31).

The *nature* of this Faith is brought out by St Paul. It is an assent of the mind to the truths of the Gospel (Rom. 10. 8–17), but it is also a free act of obedience to the Person who teaches those truths, so that man can withhold his consent if he choose (Rom. 1. 5). The act of Faith is a co-operation with divine grace and God freely makes use of it to establish man in the supernatural state of "justness" (Rom. 3. 30). In the person so "justified" it remains as a bond of union with Christ and His life-giving Passion (Gal. 2. 20). It is the foundation of Hope (Heb. 11. 1), but that does not mean that it is inactive, on the contrary it manifests itself in practical Charity (Gal. 5. 6). Since Faith is a full obedience to Christ (2 Cor. 10. 5), it involves a determination to fulfil His commands, and these commands include Baptism (Mk. 16. 16), which completes the "justifying" process begun by Faith.

The *object* of Faith is the words, work and Person of Christ. His words alone can reveal the nature of the Father (Lk. 10. 22); His redemptive work is the divinely appointed means to eternal life (Jn. 3. 14–15; cf. 12. 32–33); His Person is offered by the Father as the object of a Faith that leads to life (Jn. 6. 40). Hence the final judgment will be decided on the question of loyal belief in Him (Mt. 10. 32–33). Faith in Christ as Redeemer from sin is necessary for the individual soul if it is to secure the application of His redemption (Rom. 4.23—5.2). By means of this Faith the Gentiles enter into the blessings promised to Abraham (Rom. 4. 11–14), passing from the kingdom of Satan to the Kingdom of the Son (Col. 1. 13).

What was to become of the *Mosaic observance* in this domain of Faith? Our Lord Himself obeyed the Law and enjoined obedience to the Law even when expounded by the

Scribes and Pharisees (Mt. 23. 2–3); yet He made it clear that a change was impending. The minute observance of the Pharisees does not suffice, He says, for entrance into the Kingdom (Mt. 5. 20). He even lays down principles (Mk. 7. 14–19) which, in their logical conclusion, abrogate important Mosaic injunctions (Lev. 11. 1–47), as St Mark realizes ("Thus He made all foods clean", Mk. 7. 19, Westm. Version). Baptism and not circumcision is the external rite which, with Faith, leads to salvation (Mk. 16. 16). Jerusalem with its Temple will be destroyed (Mt. 24. 2) and so the Mosaic sacrifices will cease; a new Sacrifice is substituted (Lk. 22. 19–20). Indeed, our Lord's outlook so goes beyond the Law that we are forced to ask in what sense He could be said to "fulfil" it (Mt. 5. 17)? First, in His own Person and work, because the Law and the Prophets announced Him (Lk. 24. 44); secondly, by leading its permanent moral commands to further perfection (Mt. 5. 21–48); thirdly, by establishing this perfected law with a new authority—the authority of the Son of God; fourthly, by recalling the spirit which should have guided and dominated the observance of the Law (Deut. 6. 5; cf. Mt. 22. 34–40); lastly, by robbing the Law of what was temporary in it and what was national, He made it possible and obligatory for all ages and all nations. This perfecting process was so wide and so deep that a new era may be said to have begun: "The Law and the Prophets were until John; from that time the Kingdom of God is preached" (Lk. 16. 16).

What is the sanctifying power of Faith in the new regime, as compared with the effects of the Law in the old (cf. Phil. 3. 9)? St Paul treats of this matter at great length. He points out (and this would shock those who had been his fellow Pharisees) that it had never been God's intention to sanctify souls by means of the works of the Law (Rom. 9. 31–32; Gal. 2. 16). Not the Law (it did not yet exist!) but Faith had sanctified Abraham (Rom. 4. 1–25); sanctification

was possible for those who had no explicit knowledge of the
Law (Rom. 2. 14–15). Far from having in itself the power
to sanctify, the Law could not even give the power to ensure
its own fulfilment (Rom. 7. 5). What, then, was the purpose
of the Law? To restrain the moral consequences of Adam's
Fall by preserving in the Chosen People a full sense of moral
guilt (Rom. 7. 7 f.). This sense remained even when sad
experience showed how powerless the Law was to give
positive help against sin (Rom. 7. 14–25). These two things
together—the appreciation of the gravity of sin, and the
sad experience of sinning—were to be used, in God's design,
to produce in the Jewish heart a sense of positive *need*—a
need of the fullness of grace brought by Christ (Jn. 1. 16–17).
This was the divine plan, and it succeeded in those who
realized it as Peter did (Ac. 15. 9–11). Thus a goodly number
of Israel (the "remnant", according to the prophets, e.g.
Is. 10. 22) willingly accepted the new order of grace (Rom. 11.
5–6; cf. Ac. 2. 41). In this way, the Law was "a pedagogue
unto Christ" (Gal. 3. 24) as one who takes a child to school
and leaves him with his teacher.

ii. *Baptism*

Ceremonial washing was not unknown among the Jews
of our Lord's time. The ritual bath was practised, for
instance, as a preliminary to the reception of converts; in
this case the rite was a symbol that the old pagan way of life
had given place to the observance of the Law. St John the
Baptist used the same ceremony while giving it a deeper
significance. It was his office to prepare the way of the
Messias by reconciling sinners with God (Lk. 3. 3–6). He
sought more than the literal observance of the Law as
practised by the Pharisees (Mt. 3. 7–8), he required repentance for past faults with a purpose of future amendment.
His baptismal ceremony was not designed to produce this
state of heart, but to symbolize it and to give it the force

that all internal purposes derive from external acts connected with them. In this sense, John's baptism was "unto remission of sins". Yet John himself was fully aware of the inferiority of his own baptism when compared with the immersion in the Holy Ghost which Another was to achieve (Lk. 3. 16). This immersion was to be effected by a similar material rite (Jn. 3. 5), a rite which, with the faith which it presupposes, is a necessary condition of salvation (Mk. 16. 16) and which is regarded as such from the first days of the Apostolic preaching (Ac. 2. 38; 8. 12, 36–38; 9. 18; 10. 47–48).

Unlike the baptism of John, this new baptism effects the sanctification of the receiver (provided, of course, that his dispositions present no obstacle). This sanctification is represented as a spiritual re-birth (Jn. 3. 5), the rite is a "bath of regeneration" (Tit. 3. 5). This new life by which all the baptized live is the same in all, abolishing all distinction, even that of circumcision (Col. 3. 11), for it is the life of Christ (Gal. 3. 27). This life is not, of course, that of Christ's material body but it is equally real; it is a real spiritual force imparted by Christ and giving the power to act vigorously and meritoriously in the supernatural order. The image which this suggests to Paul is that of the human body with its one head and many members; it is the product of Baptism (1 Cor. 12. 12 f.). Our Lord Himself had used the picture of the vine with its many branches (Jn. 15. 5). It is in this very profound sense that we must understand the phrase "union with Christ". The union is brought about by Faith, but it must be a Faith—as we have seen—which contains at least a desire of Baptism. Now, both Faith and Baptism aim at a union with Christ as Redeemer, because it is by reason of Christ's Redemption that His life flows into the "members" of His "body". Baptism, therefore, unites the baptized mysteriously with the death and resurrection of our Lord:

"We were buried therefore with Him through His baptism unto death, that as Christ was raised from the dead through the glory of the Father, so we also should walk in newness of life." (Cf. Rom. 6. 3–11.)

As Christ died *for* sin so the baptized Christian is placed in a state of death *to* sin; he is thus crucified with Christ (Gal. 2. 20), dead and buried with Him (2 Tim. 2. 11; Col. 2. 12), risen to a new life with Him (Eph. 2. 5 f.), living with Him (2 Tim. 2. 11), seated with Him in heaven (Eph. 2. 6), reigning with Him (2 Tim. 2. 12).

Is Baptism, therefore, all-sufficient for salvation? No, because the "new creature" which emerges from the baptismal water (Gal. 6. 15) is "created in Christ Jesus *for good works*" (Eph. 2. 10). It is still possible for those who, by Baptism, are no longer "in the flesh but in the spirit" to thwart their new state by living "according to the flesh"— such shall surely die (cf. Rom. 8. 1–13). It is possible, then, for the new life to weaken and fail; it has need of nourishment.

iii. *The Holy Eucharist*

The purpose of Faith and Baptism is incorporation in the "mystical body" of Christ, the bringing about of that profound "union" which we have described, enabling the life of the Head to be communicated to the members. The purpose of the Holy Eucharist is to perfect and sustain that life by intensifying the union:

"He that eateth My flesh and drinketh My blood abideth in Me and I in him . . . the same also shall live by Me." (Jn. 6. 57–58.)

The Eucharist is not merely a better means of sustaining the union and the life, it is a necessary means:

"Except you eat the flesh of the Son of Man and drink His blood, you shall not have life in you." (Jn. 6. 54.)

Like Baptism, but even more closely, the Eucharist is bound up with the Passion and Death of our Lord:

"As often as you eat this Bread and drink this Chalice you shall shew the death of the Lord until He come." (1 Cor. 11. 26.)

Nor is it merely a memorial of His death, since it contains the actual Body that was given over to death and the Blood that was shed (Lk. 22. 19–20). It is, therefore, the closest union that can be conceived with the lifegiving sacrificial Victim (1 Pet. 1. 18–23) who came to give life in abundance (Jn. 10. 10).

VII. LIFE IN THE KINGDOM

How much the Kingdom of Jesus surpassed the Jewish expectations of the Messianic reign is nowhere more apparent than in the conception of the new life which He promised and conferred. The Kingdom is held together in one united whole by reason of the one common life which all share (1 Cor. 12. 13); national and social distinctions may remain (1 Cor. 7. 22) but they are barriers no longer, Jew and Gentile, slave and freeman are all one in Christ (Col. 3. 11). This living and united thing grows under the influence of its Head (Col. 2. 19), the unity and the growth being guaranteed especially by a common share in the one Food (1 Cor. 10. 16–17) and safeguarded by those who hold office in the society (Eph. 4. 11–13).

The life of the citizen in the Kingdom must be an *active* one. He must not presume that by his Baptism his ultimate salvation is assured, for if he does he falls into the error of the "sons of Abraham" (Lk. 3. 7–9); he must work out this salvation "in fear and trembling" (Phil. 2. 12). His new life, inaugurated by Faith, effected by Baptism, sustained and intensified by the Eucharist, recovered if necessary by the sacrament of Penance (Jn. 20. 23), is given to him with a purpose: it is given in order to make him capable of acts

which merit an eternal reward from a just Judge (2 Tim. 4. 8).
Herein the doctrine of Christianity recognizes the value of
"works" and in this it would seem to join with the Pharisaic
teaching. The agreement is only in appearance. The Pharisees never acknowledged that man was radically incapable
of winning sanctification by his own unaided natural
strength, but Christian teaching is founded on this very
acknowledgment. If the "good fight" can really earn "the
crown" (2 Tim. 4. 7–8) it is because the Christian has been
raised to that privileged condition by freely given divine
favour—by "grace" from God through Jesus Christ (Eph.
2. 4–9).

The *dignity* of the citizen is immense. He is of the blood
royal, son of the King. The human father communicates
his human life to his child, God communicates something
of His divine life to the members of the Kingdom. He does
so through the medium of Christ who is His Son by nature
and in whom, therefore, dwells the fullness of divine life
(Col. 2. 9). Of this fullness all have in a measure received
(Jn. 1. 16) and so become sons of God (Jn. 1. 12). This sonship is the work of Christ *through the Holy Spirit*, for the
Christian is one re-born "of the Holy Ghost" (Jn. 3. 5)
and it is by the Spirit that he continues to live (Gal. 5. 25).
This Spirit, though a distinct Divine Person (cf. e.g. Rom 8.
9) is "the Spirit of the Son" (Gal. 4. 6), because the Son
possesses Him in fullness (1 Cor. 15. 45) and is the cause of
His abundant outpouring (Jn. 16. 7). For the body of the
faithful as a whole it results that, while Christ (the sender of
the Spirit) remains the Head, the Spirit is the living and
binding principle. For the individual it means that Son and
Spirit together work his sanctification. By their common
labour the soul suffers a rich change. It now shares, as far as
its created nature will allow, in the Sonship of Christ, and
like a new-born child it cries to God "Abba", which means
"Father" (Gal. 4. 6). For this mysterious re-creation of the

soul St Paul finds the word "adoption" (Gal. 4. 4–7), and the state in which the "adopted son" finds himself is "the state of grace". Yet even this is not the end of the divine favour:

"We are now the sons of God and it hath not yet appeared what we shall be." (1 Jn. 3. 1–2.)

This "state of grace" merges into the future state of "Glory" (Jn. 4. 13 f.) when "we shall be like to Him (God) because we shall see Him even as He is" (1 Jn. 3, 2).

Nor is the body itself, partner of the soul's merits, excluded from this future state of glory. Here, too, Satan's triumph must not be final; not one outpost of the Enemy must remain, and the last outpost is death (1 Cor. 15. 26). Thus the soul that dies to sin with Christ's death finds its body risen to a new life through Christ's Resurrection. It could scarcely be otherwise since the whole human person of the faithful Christian is one with Christ and is consequently drawn into His triumph.[1]

VIII. The King

The distinctive doctrine of Christianity has now been sufficiently demonstrated: Christ is not a king aloof from His Kingdom; He is at the very heart of it, diffusing His life through His mystical body. In this very real sense, "Christianity is Christ", and any attempt to obscure this sense by questioning His divine nature or the consequently infinite power of His redemption will result in a new religion, unintended by Christ Himself, unforeseen by St Paul and the Apostles. For this reason our Lord is not the Messias of Pharisaic Judaism; He is not merely the Founder of the Kingdom, He is its very Foundation (1 Cor. 3. 11), passing His own strength to every single stone of the structure. Far exceeding the contemporary Messianic hope, He does not only remove the obstacles to the service of God but actually

[1] Cf. chapter 15 of the first Epistle to the Corinthians.

supplies the vital force which makes that service possible and meritorious. The cry: "I live, now not I but the Messias liveth in me" could never have come from an unconverted Pharisee (Gal. 2. 20).

Because this King is the origin of the spiritual life of His subjects (Ac. 3. 15) and their final goal (Rom. 14. 7–8), He is also the object of their love and hope (1 Pet. 1. 8–9) and "to be with Christ" is the final happiness (Phil. 1. 23–24). This explains the eager prayer which brings the New Testament to a close: "Come, Lord Jesus" (Apoc. 22. 20).

*   *   *   *   *   *

When earthly history is over, the Messianic King presents His dearly-won Kingdom to the Father. Victor by His own resurrection over the enemy death, He has reigned as God-man until the last fruits of the victory are gathered in the final resurrection of all men. Then His human mission is at an end, and He lays Himself and His Kingdom at the feet of the Father, though as the Son of God He sits with Him upon the eternal throne (Apoc. 22. 1–3).

"Christ the firstfruits, then they that are Christ's shall rise at His coming; then shall be the end, when He shall surrender the kingdom to God the Father, when he shall have brought to naught all other rule and all other authority and power . . . The last enemy to be brought to naught is death . . . And when all things shall be subject to Him, then shall the Son Himself be subject to the Father who subjected all things to Him, that God may be all in all." (1 Cor. 15. 23–28.)

APPROXIMATE CHRONOLOGY OF THE PROPHETIC WRITINGS

Amos	783–743 B.C.
Osee	783–721
Isaias (cc. 1–35)	740–700
Micheas	740–715
Sophonias	640–630
Jeremias	627–585
Nahum	614
Habacuc	605–597
Ezechiel	593–571
Isaias (cc. 40-55)	586–540
Isaias (cc. 56–66)	530
Aggeus	520
Zacharias (cc. 1–8)	520–518
Malachy	450
Abdias	Fifth century
Jonas	Fifth century
Joel	400
Zacharias (cc. 9–14)	300
Daniel	167–164
Baruch	Second–First century.

INDEX OF BIBLICAL TEXTS

INDEX OF NAMES AND SUBJECTS

Simon Peter, cf. Peter, St
Sin 6–7, 37, 121–122, 130, 144,
    147, 158, 172–173, 174–178,
    181
Sinai 18, 19, 20–21, 23
Sion 38, 40–42
Sion, New 60
Slaves 69, 179
Solomon 15, 40, 41, 42–43, 70, 138,
    158
Son of David, cf. Messias, Jesus
    Christ
Son of God 133, 137, 147, 153,
    154, 157, 175, (cf. Messias,
    Jesus Christ)
Son of Man 83, 104, 123, 132, 147,
    168
Sons of Abraham 179
Sons of God 159, 160, 180–181
Sons of Israel 13, 16
Soothsaying 23–24, 32
Sophonias 33, 34, 55, 58, 64–65
Sosenk, cf. Sesac
Southern Kingdom 42–46, 54, 55,
    60, 61, 62, 64, 66–68 (cf. Jews,
    Judaism)
Spirit of God 79, 81, 180
Spouse of Yahweh 54
Star of Jacob 24
Suez 19
Sun-worship 56
Superstition 23
Susa 68, 71
Symbols 92, 106, 132, 176
Synagogues 115, 126, 127, 130,
    136, 141, 158
Syria 59, 66, 70, 89, 91–97, 99, 101,
    103, 110, 112, 115, 116, 117,
    118, 119, 135
Syrians 44, 46, 47, 48
Syro-Ephraimitic coalition 47, 55

Tabernacle 40–41, 58
Tabernacles, feast of 151, 160, 161,
    163
Tabor 110
Taurus 91
Taxation 42, 118–119
Temple, Messianic 79, 84
Temple:
    of Herod 91–94, 102, 103, 109,
        114, 117–119, 126, 175
    of Onias, cf. Leontopolis

Temple:
    of Solomon 15, 41, 42, 45, 46, 55,
        56, 57, 58, 67, 73, 74, 76, 77,
        78, 85
    of Zorobabel 70–71, 72, 79, 80,
        87, 113, 114, 117, 120
Temples, pagan 113, 114, 117, 120
Temptations of Christ 149
Terah 9–10
Testament of Twelve Patriarchs
    107
Tetrarchs 111, 115
Theglathphalasar III 47
Theocracy 21, 32, 39, 90
Thomas, St 159
Tiberias 115
Tiberius 118–120
Tobiads 92
Tobias the Ammonite 72
Tolerance, religious 69, 116–117
Torah, cf. Law, Mosaic
Trachonitis 113, 115
Trance 31
Transfiguration 141, 154, 159
Transjordania 46, 47, 67, 97, 99,
    100
Trinity 143, 180–181
Tryphon 95, 96
Two-year Ministry 161
Tyre 67, 87, 96

Union with Christ, cf. Mystical
    Body
Unity of Sanctuary 41, 43
Universalism 11, 49, 50, 61–65,
    81, 82, 127, 137, 139–140,
    169–175
Ur 10

Valerius Gratus 117
Varus 115
Victim 156, 179 (cf. Sacrifice)
Virgin 62, 139, 140
Visions 30, 31
Vulgate 52

Wandering 22–23, 24
Will of God 166, 168
Wisdom, Book of 108
Wisdom literature 86, 107–109
Woman 7, 8

ANALYTICAL INDEX